ASIAN TAPAS

ASIAN TAPAS

over 60 recipes for tempting
Asian small plates and bites

RYLAND PETERS & SMALL
LONDON • NEW YORK

Senior Designer Toni Kay
Commissioning Editor Alice Sambrook
Production Controller Mai-Ling Collyer
Art Director Leslie Harrington
Editorial Director Julia Charles
Publisher Cindy Richards
Indexer Vanessa Bird

First published in 2018 by
Ryland Peters & Small
20–21 Jockey's Fields, London WC1R 4BW
and
341 E 116th St, New York NY 10029
www.rylandpeters.com

10 9 8 7 6 5 4 3 2 1

Recipe collection compiled by
Alice Sambrook

Text copyright © Valerie Aikman-Smith,
Caroline Artiss, Jordan Bourke, Dunja
Gulin, Tori Haschka, Carol Hilker, Vicky
Jones, Jackie Kearney, Jenny Linford,
Loretta Liu, Uyen Luu, Dan May, Nitisha
Patel, Louise Pickford, Milli Taylor and
Ryland Peters & Small 2018

Design and photographs copyright ©
Ryland Peters & Small 2018

ISBN: 978-1-84975-934-2

Printed in China

A CIP record for this book is available
from the British Library.

US Library of Congress Cataloging-in-
Publication Data has been applied for.

NOTES:
• Both British (Metric) and
American (Imperial plus US cups)
measurements are included in these
recipes for your convenience, however
it is important to work with one set
of measurements and not alternate
between the two within a recipe.
• All spoon measurements are level
unless otherwise specified.
• All eggs are medium (UK) or large
(US), unless specified as large, in
which case US extra-large should be
used. Uncooked or partially cooked
eggs should not be served to the very
old, frail, young children, pregnant
women or those with compromised
immune systems.
• Ovens should be preheated
to the specified temperatures.
We recommend using an oven
thermometer. If using a fan-assisted
oven, adjust temperatures according
to the manufacturer's instructions.
• When a recipe calls for the grated
zest of citrus fruit, buy unwaxed fruit
and wash well before using. If you can
only find treated fruit, scrub well in
warm soapy water before using.

CONTENTS

INTRODUCTION

Most people are familiar with the idea of tapas in Spanish bars. Originally, it was the practice of offering tempting little dishes to customers on the house to accompany their glass of wine or an ice-cold draft beer, but it is now more widely understood to be a style of dining that involves sharing small plates with others. And this idea of sharing food is not exclusive to Europe. In Japan, bars known as 'izakaya' offer an informal place to enjoy an after-work drink with something small to eat. And unlike other Japanese styles of eating, the dishes in these venues are usually shared by everyone at the table, just like tapas. The modern concept of Asian tapas fuses the unbeatable appeal of socializing over small-portion sharing plates with the more exotic and enticing flavours of Asian cuisine. It offers a multitude of delicious possibilities for tasty dishes and another way to entertain your friends at home in style.

In this mouth-watering collection of recipes you will find ideas for bite-size morsels from Asian cuisines as diverse as China, Japan, Korea, Vietnam, Thailand and India. A chapter of recipes for irresistible Parcels, Rolls & Dumplings includes perfect fingerfood ideas from egg rolls and bao buns to dim sum and wontons. Fritters, Frys & Pancakes make a more substantial snack. Choose from filled crispy pancakes, bhajis, dosas and pakoras. Lighter Bites on offer, such as summer rolls, sushi and tempura are ideal served as little teasers in advance of an Asian-style feast. And if you want to lay on a full sharing menu, choose something from Ribs, Grills & Wings such as sticky Korean ribs, Vietnamese BBQ ribs or Indian grilled lamb chops as the star of the show. With meat, fish and vegetarian options included, it's also possible to create an informal dinner or a feast for a crowd that offers something for everyone.

It makes sense to consider what you serve to drink with your nibbles. A good accompaniment to dim sum, fluffy buns or dumplings is a tea that will cut through any oiliness. Try a black tea such as Pu-Erh tea, a so-called 'blue tea' like Oolong, or a green tea like Dragonwell. And if you prefer a herbal infusion, look in your local Asian market for Chrysanthemum tea which is mild and much like camomile. For sushi, a fresh and fruity sake is the best choice. Although traditionally served warm, most premium sake produced these days tastes better slightly chilled, just like wine. Serve it in little ceramic cups for authenticity! Cold bottled beer is a great choice for grilled sticky ribs and wings, and there are plenty of excellent Asian brands to choose from. Look for India's Cobra beer or Singha lager, or for a Japanese theme, choose Asahi or Sapporo or even a Korean Cass.

Choose your dishes, pair them with something good to wash it all down with and enjoy the Asian tapas experience at home!

BASIC DOUGH RECIPES

WHEAT DOUGH

150 g/1 cup plus 2 tablespoons Asian white
    wheat flour
80 ml/scant ⅓ cup water

MAKES 16 DUMPLING SKINS

Place the flour in a mixing bowl and mix
together with the water to form a dough. Turn
the dough out onto a lightly floured surface and
knead for 20–25 minutes or until the dough
is smooth and elastic. Separate and roll into
two equal cylinders about 2.5 cm/1 inch in
diameter. Cover with a damp kitchen cloth to
prevent from drying out and set aside to rest
at room temperature for 30 minutes.

Use a sharp knife to slice the dough cylinders
into 16 equal pieces. On a lightly floured surface,
roll out each piece with a rolling pin until it has
a neat round shape and a diameter of around
7.5 cm/3 inches.

EGG DOUGH

150 g/1 cup plus 2 tablespoons Asian white
    wheat flour
40 ml/3 tablespoons water
1 egg

MAKES 16 DUMPLING SKINS

Place the flour in a mixing bowl and add the
water and egg. Mix together, then turn the
dough out onto a lightly floured surface. Using
lightly floured hands, knead for 20–25 minutes.
The dough will be sticky at first but will become
smooth and silky. Separate in half and roll into
two equal cylinders, each about 2.5 cm/1 inch

in diameter. Cover with a damp kitchen cloth
and set aside to rest at room temperature for
30 minutes.

Use a sharp knife to slice the dough cylinders
into 16 equal pieces. On a lightly floured
surface, roll out each piece with a rolling
pin until it has a neat round shape and
a diameter of around 7.5 cm/3 inches.

PUFF PASTRY DOUGH

WATER DOUGH
100 g/¾ cup Asian white wheat flour
15 g/1 heaped tablespoon caster/superfine sugar
40 ml/3 tablespoons water
30 g/2 tablespoons unsalted butter, melted

BUTTER DOUGH
100 g/¾ cup Asian white wheat flour
50 g/3½ tablespoons unsalted butter, melted

MAKES 12 DUMPLING SKINS

In a mixing bowl, combine all the ingredients
for the water dough. Form the dough into a ball
and knead lightly until smooth and silky. Wrap
the dough in clingfilm/plastic wrap and rest
in the fridge for 15 minutes. Divide into 12 and
roll each piece into a ball. Cover with a damp
kitchen cloth and set aside.

In a second mixing bowl, repeat the same full
process with the butter dough ingredients but
instead of chilling, rest at room temperature
for 15 minutes.

Take a water dough ball and knead gently and
briefly. Very lightly flour the worktop and use
a rolling pin to roll out the ball of water dough
to a diameter of 7.5 cm/3 inches. Place a

butter dough ball in the centre and wrap the water dough around to enclose it completely. Turn the dough ball over so the join is on the underside. Roll the combined dough into a thick square parcel. Fold the parcel into three and flatten with the rolling pin again. Repeat this fold and roll process twice with each ball. Cover and rest in the fridge for 15 minutes before rolling into the desired shape for the recipe.

BREAD DOUGH

2 teaspoons fast-action dried yeast
450 g/3½ cups Asian white wheat flour
100 g/¾ cup plus 1 tablespoon icing/
confectioners' sugar, sifted
15 g/2 tablespoons dried milk powder
¼ teaspoon fine salt
2 teaspoons baking powder
180 ml/¾ cup water, add more if needed
50 ml/scant ¼ cup vegetable oil, plus extra
for oiling the bowl

MAKES 16 BAO BUNS

Place the yeast in a large mixing bowl, then add the flour, sugar, milk powder, salt and baking powder. Make sure the yeast is separated from the salt by the layer of flour. Add the water and oil and bring together with a dough scraper. When no dry flour remains, remove the dough from the bowl and place on a lightly floured surface. Knead firmly for 5–10 minutes, until smooth and elastic.

Lightly oil the mixing bowl. Shape the dough into two cylinders and place back in the oiled bowl, cover with oiled clingfilm/plastic wrap and leave in a warm place to rise for 40–60 minutes or until doubled in size.

Remove the risen dough from the bowl, punch it down and knead it again briefly, but very carefully rather than firmly this time. Roll the dough out into a big rectangle and portion it out into 16 equal balls. Cover the dough balls with oiled clingfilm/plastic wrap and leave to rest again for 30 minutes in a warm place.

Roll out each dough ball so that it has a diameter of around 7.5 cm/3 inches; try to make the centre slightly thicker than the edges so that it can hold the filling. Cover each dough circle with a damp kitchen cloth as you finish to stop it from drying out.

CRYSTAL SKIN DOUGH

100 g/¾ cup wheat starch
50 g/½ cup tapioca starch
pinch of salt
150 ml/⅔ cup boiling (not hot) water

MAKES 16 DUMPLING SKINS

Combine the wheat starch, tapioca starch and salt in a large bowl. Add the boiling water and mix with a wooden spoon to form the dough. Transfer to a lightly floured surface and knead until smooth. Separate the dough in half and roll into two equal cylinders, about 2.5 cm/ 1 inch in diameter. Wrap in clingfilm/plastic wrap and rest at room temperature for 30 minutes.

Divide the dough into 16 equal balls. On a lightly floured surface use a rolling pin to roll the dough balls into thin discs, about 5 cm/ 2 inches in diameter. Cover the finished skins with a damp kitchen cloth as you work so that they don't dry out.

PARCELS, ROLLS
& DUMPLINGS

CHINESE EGG ROLLS

There is something so satisfying about an egg roll. Maybe it's the crunch; maybe it's the texture; maybe it's something about how pork and cabbage come together so well when hugged between egg roll wrappers and deep-fried. Whatever it is, they're delicious!

3 tablespoons olive oil
1 teaspoon sea salt
1 teaspoon freshly ground
    black pepper
1 teaspoon ground ginger
1 teaspoon garlic powder
450 g/1 lb. pork shoulder
2 tablespoons plain/
    all-purpose flour
2 tablespoons water
120 g/2 cups cabbage,
    shredded
1 medium carrot, shredded
8 x 18-cm/7-inch square egg
    roll wrappers
1 litre/quart peanut oil,
    for frying
2 tablespoons toasted
    sesame seeds (optional)

SWEET & SOUR
DIPPING SAUCE
1 tablespoon soy sauce
1 tablespoon water
3½ tablespoons caster/
    superfine sugar
3½ tablespoons white vinegar
zest of 1 unwaxed orange

meat thermometer

MAKES 8

Preheat the oven to 180°C (350°F) Gas 4.

Rub the oil, salt, ground black pepper, ginger and garlic powder onto the pork shoulder.

Set the meat on a rack set into a roasting pan. Roast for 20 minutes, and then reduce the heat to 160°C (325°F) Gas 3. Continue to cook until a meat thermometer inserted into the shoulder reads 85°C (185°F), about 1–2 hours. Remove the pork from the oven and let stand until cool enough to handle, about 30 minutes. Shred the pork.

Combine the flour and water in a bowl until they form a paste. In a separate bowl combine the cabbage, carrot and shredded pork and mix them together.

Lay out one egg roll wrapper with a corner pointed toward you.

Place about 20 g/⅓ cup of the cabbage, carrot and shredded pork mixture onto the wrapper and fold the corner up over the mixture.

Fold the left and right corners toward the centre and continue to roll. Brush a bit of the flour paste on the final corner to help seal.

In a large frying pan/skillet, heat the peanut oil to about 190°C (375°F). Place the egg rolls into the heated oil and fry, turning occasionally, until golden brown. Remove from oil and drain on paper towels. Put on a serving plate and top with toasted sesame seeds, if desired.

To make the sweet and sour sauce, mix all the ingredients together in a mixing bowl. Transfer to a small saucepan and bring to the boil, then remove from the heat. Pour the sauce into a small bowl ready to dip the egg rolls into.

TAIWANESE-STYLE GARLIC PORK BAO

Pillowy Taiwanese-style buns contrast beautifully with the gutsy, succulent braised pork, making these a memorably tasty treat.

BRAISED PORK
1 tablespoon olive oil
1 onion, finely chopped
2 garlic cloves, chopped
2-cm/¾-inch fresh ginger, peeled and chopped
400 g/14 oz. pork belly, cut into 2.5-cm/1-inch cubes
1 tablespoon Korean soy bean paste
1 tablespoon Korean chilli paste
1 tablespoon dark soy sauce
1 tablespoon rice wine or medium sherry
1 teaspoon white sugar
300 ml/1¼ cups chicken stock or water

BAO (TAIWANESE BUNS)
250 g/1¾ cups plain/ all-purpose flour
2 teaspoons white sugar
½ teaspoon fast-action dried yeast
½ teaspoon baking powder
¼ teaspoon salt
100 ml/⅓ cup hand-hot water
50 ml/3½ tablespoons whole milk
2 teaspoons white wine vinegar
shredded carrot and spring onion/scallion, to garnish

large frying pan/skillet or casserole dish with a lid

bamboo steamer, lined with non-stick baking parchment

MAKES 8

First make the braised pork. Heat the oil in the large, lidded frying pan/ skillet or casserole dish. Fry the onion, garlic and ginger for 2 minutes, stirring, until the onion has softened. Add the chopped pork belly and fry, stirring often, until the pork is lightly browned.

Add the soy bean and chilli pastes and mix to coat thoroughly. Add the soy sauce, rice wine and sugar and cook, stirring, for 1 minute. Next, add the stock or water and bring to the boil.

Cover with a lid, reduce the heat and simmer for 1 hour until the pork is tender. Uncover the pan, increase the heat to bring the liquid to the boil and cook uncovered over medium heat, stirring often, until the sauce has considerably reduced. Set aside until needed.

Meanwhile, to make the bao, mix together the flour, sugar, yeast, baking powder and salt in a large bowl. Add in the hand-hot water, milk and vinegar and mix together to form a soft dough. Knead for 10 minutes until the dough is supple and smooth.

Place the dough in an oiled bowl, cover with oiled clingfilm/plastic wrap and set aside in a warm place for an hour to rise.

On a lightly floured surface, knock back the risen dough and roll to form a thick sausage shape. Cut into 8 even-sized pieces and shape each piece into a ball. Roll each ball into an oval, roughly 12-cm/5-inches long. Fold each oval in half over a small rectangular piece of baking parchment. Cover with oiled clingfilm/plastic wrap and set aside to rest for 20 minutes.

Steam the buns in batches in the bamboo steamer, spaced apart, for 10 minutes or until cooked through. Handling the hot buns carefully, remove the baking parchment.

Reheat the braised pork until piping hot, if needed, and fill each bun with braised pork, garnish with shredded carrot and spring onion/ scallion and serve at once.

MUSHROOM PUFF PASTRY DUMPLINGS

These delicious dumplings are filled with a mixture of button, shiitake and oyster mushrooms, but you can adapt the combination to suit what is available. If you can find them, shiitake mushrooms add a nice umami-like depth of flavour.

1 batch of Puff Pastry Dough,
   see page 8
2 shallots, chopped
1 garlic clove, chopped
1 teaspoon grated fresh ginger
4 button mushrooms, sliced
4 shiitake mushrooms, sliced
4 oyster mushrooms, sliced
2 spring onions/scallions,
   sliced
1 egg, beaten
salt and freshly ground
   black pepper
black sesame seeds,
   to garnish

*2 large baking sheets,
   greased*

MAKES 12

Prepare the puff pastry dough following the instructions in the basic recipe on page 8 and rest the balls in the fridge until needed.

Preheat the oven to 200°C (400°F) Gas 6.

In a small frying pan/skillet, fry the shallots over a medium heat for a few minutes until fragrant. Add the garlic and ginger and stir-fry together for a couple of minutes. Add the sliced mushrooms and spring onions/scallions and season with salt and pepper. Fry until the mushrooms are cooked and the mixture is dry. Set aside to cool.

Roll each pastry ball into a rectangle 10 x 6 cm/4 x 2½ inches.

Put a small tablespoon of filling on one side of a skin, brush the edges with beaten egg and fold in half to enclose the filling. Use a fork to make indentations and tightly seal the edges. Repeat with the rest of the dough and filling to make 12 dumplings.

Spread the parcels out on the greased baking sheets, brush the tops with beaten egg and sprinkle with black sesame seeds to garnish. Bake in the preheated oven for 20–25 minutes or until golden brown. Serve warm.

GOLDEN PUMPKIN & LEEK DUMPLINGS

Vegetables take centre-stage in these warming, golden-coloured pumpkin
and leek parcels. The interior of the dumpling should be soft in texture,
and is flavoured beautifully with Chinese chives, ginger and Sichuan pepper.
The egg dough provides just a little bite.

1 batch of Egg Dough,
   see page 8
100 g/3½ oz. firm tofu,
   drained and sliced into
   small cubes
pinch of salt
40 g/¼ cup steamed pumpkin
1 leek, finely chopped
2 Chinese chive stalks,
   white parts removed,
   finely chopped
2 Chinese cabbage leaves,
   finely chopped
handful of freshly chopped
   coriander/cilantro
1 teaspoon grated fresh ginger
1 teaspoon Sichuan pepper
1 teaspoon black pepper
2 tablespoons vegetarian
   stir-fry sauce
2 tablespoons sesame oil
black vinegar, for dipping

MAKES 16

Prepare the egg dough following the instructions in the basic recipe on page 8.

While the dough is resting, make the filling. Lightly salt the tofu slices and set them aside for 30 minutes. After that, press out as much excess water as possible paper towels.

In a large bowl, mix together the steamed pumpkin with the tofu, chopped vegetables, coriander/cilantro, ginger, Sichuan pepper, black pepper, vegetarian stir-fry sauce and sesame oil. Chill in the fridge for 30 minutes.

Roll out the egg dough, continuing to follow the instructions on page 8. Put a large teaspoon of filling into the centre of each skin. Dab a little water on one edge of the skin, fold in half over the filling and pinch the corners together to seal. Fold small pleats to seal up the middle. Continue with the rest of the batch, leaving the prepared dumplings on a tray lightly dusted with flour and covered with a damp kitchen cloth as you work.

Put a large pan of water on to boil. Lower the dumplings into the boiling water and cover with a lid. As soon as they start to float, they are cooked. Serve hot with black vinegar for dipping.

Alternatively, you can lightly pan-fry the uncooked dumpling and finish off the cooking by poaching the dumplings in a little stock or water.

CHINESE VEGETABLE CLAMSHELL BUNS

The fashionable clamshell shape of these buns shows off the vibrant colours of the vegetables. Take care with preparation as your knife skills will be on show. These buns are also good stuffed with the braised pork on page 15.

1 batch of Bread Dough, see page 9
1 head of Chinese cabbage leaves
3 handfuls Chinese spinach
2 small leeks
1 carrot, peeled and grated
8 oyster mushrooms, sliced
3 Chinese chive stalks, white parts removed, sliced
2 tablespoons sunflower oil, plus extra for oiling the dough
large handful of freshly chopped coriander/cilantro
vegetarian stir-fry sauce, to serve

bamboo steamer, lined with non-stick baking parchment

MAKES 16

Prepare, rise and roll out the bread dough following the instructions in the basic recipe on page 9.

Divide the dough into 16 round balls and flatten each slightly with a rolling pin into an oval shape, around 12 x 6 cm/4 ½ x 2 ⅓ inches. Cut 16 squares of baking parchment, each 12 cm/4 ½ inches. Use your fingers to lightly oil the surface of a piece of dough, place a square of paper on top and fold the dough in half so that the paper is in the centre. Cut another 16 squares of baking parchment just larger than the buns. Lay the paper squares on a tray and lightly dust with flour. Place a bun on top of each square on its side, cover with oiled clingfilm/plastic wrap and leave to rise for 30–40 minutes.

While the buns are rising, slice the cabbage leaves, spinach and leeks lengthwise into ribbons approximately 6 cm/2¼ inches long and 2 cm/¾ inch thick. Set aside.

Brush the top of each risen bun lightly with sunflower oil. Lift the buns on their squares and place in the bamboo steamer about 4 cm/ 1½ inches apart. Steam over boiling water for 15–20 minutes until light and fluffy.

Heat the sunflower oil in a wok and stir-fry all the vegetables and herbs for around 2–3 minutes. Add vegetarian stir-fry sauce to taste and give the vegetables a quick toss.

When the buns are ready, remove the baking parchment from the middle of each one and fill with the hot vegetables. Serve.

SALMON & MUSHROOM DUMPLINGS

Salmon is a popular ingredient in any cuisine. It works well with the light texture of a crystal skin dough and the pink against the white is attractive.

1 batch of Crystal Skin Dough, see page 9
1 oyster mushroom
1 bunch enoki mushrooms
3 shiitaki mushrooms
20 g/¼ cup chanterelle mushrooms
1 tablespoon sunflower oil
1 garlic clove, finely chopped
1 small salmon fillet
1 tablespoon grated fresh ginger
1 bunch of Chinese chive stalks, white parts removed
chilli/chile oil, to serve

small round pastry cutter

bamboo steamer, lined with non-stick baking parchment

MAKES 12

Prepare the crystal skin dough following the basic recipe on page 9, and make the filling while the dough is resting.

Slice the mushrooms into small, even pieces. Heat the sunflower oil in a pan/skillet and fry the mushrooms and garlic over a medium heat until fragrant. Set aside to cool, discarding any excess juice.

Roll out the crystal skin dough and stamp out 24 circles using the small round pastry cutter. Portion the salmon fillet into 12 pieces and cut the Chinese chive stalks into 3-cm/2-inch lengths.

Place a salmon piece in the centre of a skin, add a sprinkle of grated ginger and a chive piece neatly on the top. Lastly, top with a teaspoon of the cooked mushrooms. Cover with another round skin and press around the edge to seal.

Place the dumplings into the lined bamboo steamer and steam over boiling water until transparent and the salmon is cooked through. Serve hot with chilli/chile oil for dipping.

FRIED SHRIMP & SCALLOP BAO

These bread buns are intensely delicious yet classy comfort food. With the surprise of a whole scallop in the centre, they are sure to be a winner. Separate dipping sauces are not usually needed with bread buns such as these as the filling inside should be juicy enough.

1 batch of Bread Dough, see page 9
2 spring onions/scallions, chopped
¼ head of cabbage, chopped
400 g/14 oz. raw prawns/shrimp, peeled and deveined
3 tablespoons oyster sauce
2 tablespoons Korean chilli flakes/hot red pepper flakes
1 tablespoon sesame oil
2 tablespoons Shaoxing rice wine
16 raw, fresh scallops

bamboo steamer, lined with non-stick baking parchment

MAKES 16

Make the bread dough following the instructions from the basic recipe on page 9, and leave to rise while you prepare the filling.

Mix the spring onions/scallions and cabbage together in a large bowl. Mince the prawns/shrimp by chopping them very finely with a sharp knife. Add these to the vegetables along with the oyster sauce, chilli flakes/hot red pepper flakes, sesame oil and Shaoxing rice wine. Mix together well and chill in the fridge.

Continue to follow the instructions from the bread dough recipe on page 9. Once the skins are ready, place 1 tablespoon of the prawn/shrimp filling in the centre of each and add a scallop on top. Pull and pleat the edges of the dough to enclose the filling and pinch to seal the tops of the buns. Cover with oiled clingfilm/plastic wrap and let rise for a final 30 minutes.

Set the buns in the lined bamboo steamer about 5 cm/2 inches apart. You may have to do this in batches depending on the size of your bamboo steamer.

Steam the buns over boiling water for 8–10 minutes until the dough is light and fluffy and the scallop inside is cooked. Let cool slightly and serve warm.

SCALLOP & CRAB DUMPLINGS

The scallop is the opalescent jewel in the crown of these dumplings, which are great for impressing guests at a dinner party. The spicy lime-based dipping sauce is the perfect complement to the luxurious seafood filling.

1 batch of Crystal Skin Dough, see page 9
1 leek, finely chopped
60 g/2¼ oz. fresh mixed white and brown crab meat, flaked
1 teaspoon grated fresh ginger
1 teaspoon crushed garlic
½ teaspoon salt
½ teaspoon ground white pepper
½ teaspoon Shaoxing rice wine
½ teaspoon white sugar
1 teaspoon oil
1 teaspoon cornflour/cornstarch
16 raw, fresh scallops

DIPPING SAUCE
4 tablespoons sugar
2 tablespoons water
2 tablespoons white vinegar
1 garlic clove, crushed
1 tablespoon fish sauce
1 teaspoon Indonesian chilli/chile sauce
freshly squeezed juice of 2 limes
handful of freshly chopped coriander/cilantro

bamboo steamer, lined with non-stick baking parchment

MAKES 16

Begin by making the dipping sauce. Boil the sugar, water and vinegar in a small saucepan until the sugar has dissolved. Turn down the heat to medium, stir in the garlic, fish sauce and chili/chile sauce and simmer for 1 minute. Remove from the heat. Cool and add the lime juice and coriander/cilantro. Set aside ready for later.

Prepare the crystal dough following the instructions in the basic recipe on page 9. While the dough is resting make the filling. In a bowl combine the leek, crab meat, ginger, garlic, seasoning, Shaoxing rice wine, sugar, oil and cornflour/cornstarch; mix well.

Roll out the crystal dough skins, continuing to follow the instructions on page 9. Put a large teaspoon of the crab mixture into the centre of each skin and place a scallop on the top. Fold the skin in half over the filling, and pinch together the sides to create the traditional crescent shaped dumpling. Fold the two ends of the crescent inwards so that they overlap. Press together to seal and form the Chinese ingot shape.

Place the dumplings into the lined bamboo steamer. Steam over boiling water for 15–20 minutes or until the skin is transparent. Serve the dumplings hot with the dipping sauce.

TRADITIONAL SHRIMP DUMPLINGS

Also known as *har gao*, these little dumplings are one of the most iconic dim sum dishes. The crystal skin should be delicate enough to just about see the pink shrimp peeping through.

1 batch of Crystal Skin Dough, see page 9
50 g/1¾ oz. firm tofu, drained and excess water pressed out
150 g/5¼ oz. raw prawns/shrimp, peeled and deveined
1 teaspoon minced fresh ginger
1 teaspoon crushed garlic
½ teaspoon Shaoxing rice wine
½ teaspoon salt
½ teaspoon sugar
½ teaspoon ground white pepper
1 teaspoon olive oil
1 teaspoon cornflour/cornstarch

DIPPING SAUCE
1 small piece fresh ginger, peeled and finely sliced
6 tablespoons black vinegar

bamboo steamer lined with non-stick baking parchment

MAKES 16

Finely mince the drained tofu using a sharp knife.

Chop each prawn/shrimp into 4–5 small pieces and place in a bowl. Add the drained and minced tofu, ginger, garlic, Shaoxing rice wine, salt, sugar, white pepper, oil, and cornflour/cornstarch. Mix well and set aside in the fridge to marinate while you make the dough.

Prepare, rest and then roll out the crystal skin dough following the instructions in the basic recipe on page 9. Place a large teaspoon of filling neatly into the centre of a skin. Fold the skin in half over the filling. Pinch one end together and start to crimp the edge by making small folds to form pleats to create the traditional crescent shape.

Put the dumplings into the lined bamboo steamer. Steam over boiling water for 15–20 minutes or until the skin is transparent and the prawns/shrimp are red.

To make the dipping sauce, stir the sliced ginger into the black vinegar. Serve the dumplings hot alongside the dipping sauce.

LOTUS LEAF RICE DUMPLINGS

The lotus is considered a sacred plant in Chinese culture, the fruit of which is delicious but hard to find. More prevalent are the giant strong-textured leaves, perfect for holding filling but still pleasant to eat.

370 g/2 cups sweet glutinous/sticky rice
4 dried lotus leaves
½ teaspoon salt
1 teaspoon sesame oil
1 chicken breast, finely chopped
1 tablespoon cornflour/cornstarch
2 teaspoons vegetable oil
4 shiitake mushrooms, sliced
1 leek, sliced
1 Chinese sausage (marinated and smoked pork sausage found in Chinese markets), thinly sliced
2 teaspoons oyster sauce
2 teaspoons soy sauce
1 tablespoon Shaoxing rice wine
2 tablespoons caster/superfine sugar

rice cooker

bamboo steamer, lined with non-stick baking parchment

MAKES 8

Rinse and drain the rice, then soak in 600 ml/2½ cups water for 2 hours.

Meanwhile, fold and cut each lotus leaf in half lengthways. Submerge the leaves in hot water and leave to soak for 30 minutes, pressing down if they float up. Trim the leaves with kitchen scissors/shears until they are a similar size and trim off the hard stalk end.

Drain the rice thoroughly. In the bowl of a rice cooker, place the rice, salt, sesame oil and 250 ml/1 cup water. Cook following the packet instructions.

Mix the chopped chicken with the cornflour/cornstarch. Put the vegetable oil in a large frying pan/skillet over a high heat and fry the chicken for 3 minutes. Add the mushrooms, sliced leek and sausage and cook, stirring, for a further few minutes. Lower the heat and add the oyster sauce, soy sauce, Shaoxing rice wine and caster/superfine sugar. Stir-fry until chicken is cooked and the vegetables are tender. Set aside to cool.

Divide the cooked rice into 8 portions. With wet fingertips, divide each portion of rice in half. Shape 8 half-portions into rectangles in the centre of each lotus leaf half. Put 1 tablespoon of chicken mixture on top and spread evenly. Top the meat with the other halves of rice to cover them completely.

Fold the bottom of the leaves up over the rice. Fold in the left and right sides, and then roll each leaf away from you towards the curved edge to make a rectangular packet. Place the dumplings seam-side down on the bamboo steamer. Steam over boiling water for 45 minutes, or until heated through. Serve warm.

RED THAI CURRY & LENTIL BAO

A fragrant taste of Thailand is fused with traditional Chinese bao buns in these beautiful red curry buns.

1 batch of Bread Dough,
  see page 9
2 tablespoons sunflower oil
2 onions, finely sliced
2 garlic cloves, crushed
1–2 tablespoons Thai red
  curry paste (to taste)
2 raw chicken breasts,
  cut into bite-size pieces
500 ml/2 cups hot chicken
  stock
80 g/scant ½ cup dried
  red lentils

*bamboo steamer, lined
  with non-stick baking
  parchment*

MAKES 16

Make the bread dough following the instructions in the basic recipe on page 9. While the dough is rising, prepare the filling.

Heat 1 tablespoon of the oil in a large frying pan/skillet and add the onions. Cook for 3 minutes over a gentle heat until soft and fragrant. Stir in the garlic and curry paste and cook for 1–2 minutes more.

Add the chicken pieces and cook for 2–3 minutes. Stir in the stock and lentils, bring to the boil, cover and simmer for 25 minutes, stirring occasionally, until the lentils are tender and the chicken is cooked. Set aside to cool.

Continue to follow the instructions from the bread dough recipe on page 9.

Once the skins are ready, place 1 tablespoon of the filling in the centre of each round. Gather and pleat the edges, pinching to seal the top of the bun. Cover the finished buns with oiled clingfilm/plastic wrap and allow to rise for another 30 minutes.

Set the buns in the lined bamboo steamer about 5 cm/2 inches apart. You may have to do this in batches depending on the size of your steamer.

Once risen, steam the bao over a high heat for 15–20 minutes or until the dough is light and fluffy. Leave to cool slightly and serve.

SPICY CHICKEN & SHRIMP DUMPLINGS

A simple and delicious favourite served with a garlic, ginger and chilli/ chile oil. These are the classic flavours of Asia. The amount of hot pepper powder can be added more or less to taste.

1 batch of Wheat Dough,
  see page 8
1 chicken breast
60 g/2¼ oz. raw prawns/
  shrimp, peeled and
  deveined
1 leek, chopped
2 Chinese chive stalks,
  chopped
a large handful of freshly
  chopped coriander/cilantro
½–1 tablespoon Korean hot
  pepper powder (to taste)
1 teaspoon freshly ground
  black pepper
1 tablespoon oyster sauce
½ tablespoon sesame oil

DIPPING SAUCE
1 garlic clove, finely chopped
1 tablespoon grated fresh
  ginger
6 tablespoons soy sauce
2 tablespoons chilli/chile oil

MAKES 16

Prepare the wheat dough following the instructions in the basic recipe on page 8, and rest wrapped in clingfilm/plastic wrap until needed. Meanwhile, mince the chicken breast and prawns/shrimp using a sharp knife to very finely chop. Transfer to a mixing bowl and combine with the rest of the filling ingredients. Chill in the fridge for 30 minutes.

Roll out the skins, continuing to follow the basic recipe on page 8. Put a large teaspoon of filling into the centre of each skin. Dip your fingertips in a small dish of water and slightly moisten the edge of half the skin. Seal the dumpling up tightly using your fingers to pinch, pull and fold the skin into 4 pleats at the join. Repeat the process until all the mixture and skins have been used.

Bring a large pan of water to the boil. Gently lower in the dumplings and cover with a lid to poach. The dumplings are cooked when they float to the top of the liquid.

To make the dipping sauce, mix together all the ingredients. Drain the dumplings and serve at once accompanied with the dipping sauce.

If you prefer a crispy base, you can lightly pan-fry the uncooked dumplings in a small amount of oil and finish off the cooking by poaching in water or stock.

HOISIN DUCK PUFFS

Here, slow-cooked juicy confit duck is flavoured with five-spice, star anise, cinnamon and cloves, and enclosed in puff pastry to make these delectable treats.

1 batch of Puff Pastry Dough, see page 8
2 duck legs
60 g/¼ cup sea salt flakes, plus extra for serving
1 tablespoon freshly ground black pepper
1 garlic clove, crushed
2 tablespoons Chinese five-spice powder
5 star anise
1 cinnamon stick
2 cloves
500 g/1 lb. duck fat
2 spring onions/scallions, chopped
2 tablespoons hoisin sauce
1 egg, beaten
white sesame seeds, to garnish

small round pastry cutter

2 large baking sheets, greased

MAKES 12

Rub the duck legs with the sea salt flakes, black pepper, crushed garlic clove, five-spice powder, star anise, cinnamon stick and cloves. Pack the duck and these ingredients tightly into a dish, skin-side down. Cover the dish with clingfilm/plastic wrap and leave to marinate in the fridge for 24 hours.

Preheat the oven to 150°C (300°F) Gas 2.

Scrape the marinade off the duck pieces. Heat the duck fat in an ovenproof dish until melted, then add the duck legs, ensuring they are completely submerged.

Bake the duck in the preheated oven for 3½ hours, or until the meat is very tender when pierced with a skewer and the fat in the skin is rendered. Once cooked, remove the duck from the fat and allow to cool uncovered. Shred finely and mix with the chopped spring onions/scallions and hoisin sauce.

Prepare and roll out the puff pastry dough following the instructions from the basic recipe on page 8. Using a small round pastry cutter, stamp out 2 rounds from each dough ball portion. Put a spoonful of filling on one half, brush the edges with beaten egg and position the second piece of pastry on top. Use a fork to make indentations around the edge to tightly seal.

Preheat the oven to 200°C (400°F) Gas 6.

Brush the tops with beaten egg and sprinkle with white sesame seeds. Place on the prepared baking sheets and bake in the preheated oven for 20–25 minutes until golden brown.

BEEF BULGOGI PUFFS

Translating literally as 'fire meat' in Korean, beef bulgogi is a flavoursome dish of marinated grilled beef. The recipe was introduced to China by the migrant population of Korea. Using a good cut of beef here is key; you want the meat to be almost as soft as the flaky pastry on the outside.

1 batch of Puff Pastry Dough, see page 8
4 spring onions/scallions finely chopped
½ onion, finely chopped
¼ pineapple (pear or kiwi will also work), finely chopped
1 tablespoon dark soy sauce
1 tablespoon sugar
1 teaspoon sesame oil
freshly ground black pepper
2 garlic cloves, crushed
1 tablespoon freshly squeezed lemon juice
150 g/5¼ oz. sirloin steak, sliced into bite-size strips
1 egg, beaten
white sesame seeds, to garnish
chilli/chile sauce, for dipping

stove top griddle pan/grill pan, lightly greased

2 large baking sheets, greased

MAKES 12

Stir together the filling ingredients, apart from the meat, in a large bowl to form a marinade paste, adding a little water to loosen if necessary.

Mix the beef strips with the paste, making sure that each strip is well coated. Leave in the fridge to marinate for at least 30 minutes and up to 2 hours; left longer than this the beef may become too salty.

While the meat is marinating, prepare the 12 puff pastry dough balls following the instructions in the basic recipe on page 8. Chill in the fridge until needed.

Heat a griddle/grill pan over a medium-high heat, add the beef strips and juices to the pan and cook until the meat is browned around the edges and cooked to your liking, around 3–7 minutes. Remove from the pan and leave to cool.

Preheat the oven to 200°C (400°F) Gas 6.

Roll each pastry ball into a square about 10 cm/4 inches along each edge. Put a tablespoon of filling in the middle and brush the edges with a little beaten egg. Fold the pastry in half diagonally to create a triangle. Seal the edges then tuck the seams underneath to create a smooth finish on top. Repeat with the remaining dough and filling.

Place the puffs on the greased baking sheets and brush with beaten egg. Sprinkle with sesame seeds and bake in the preheated oven for 20–25 minutes until golden brown. Serve with the chilli/chile dipping sauce on the side.

BARBECUE PORK PUFFS

Light flaky pastry is here the yin to the yang of the dark and rich barbecue pork.
The Chinese way of making puff pastry using combined butter dough and water
dough originates from Hong Kong, and it's a little healthier than the Western
way of packing in as much butter as possible.

1 batch of Puff Pastry Dough,
   see page 8
1 tablespoon sunflower oil
1 shallot, chopped
2 tablespoons dry sherry
225 g/8 oz. pork loin, diced
1 teaspoon crushed garlic
2 tablespoons honey
2 tablespoons hoisin sauce
1 teaspoon Chinese five-spice
   powder
1 tablespoon soy sauce
1 egg, beaten
black sesame seeds,
   to garnish

heat-proof casserole dish

2 large baking sheets,
   greased

MAKES 12

For the filling, heat the oil in the heat-proof casserole dish and add the
chopped shallot. Cook until softened and lightly caramelized, about
5–7 minutes. Pour in the sherry and let the alcohol cook out. Lower the
heat to medium and add in the diced pork. Cook, stirring, for an extra
2 minutes or until lightly browned.

Meanwhile, mix the garlic, honey, hoisin sauce, five-spice powder and
soy sauce in a bowl with 2 tablespoons of water. Add this to the pork
and shallot, stirring well. Cover and cook for 1 hour over a low heat until
the sauce has thickened and the pork is soft. Check occasionally during
cooking to ensure the sauce does not dry out, adding a little extra
water if needed.

While the pork is cooking, prepare the puff pastry dough balls following
the instructions from the basic recipe on page 8. Chill in the fridge until
ready to cook.

Preheat the oven to 200°C (400°F) Gas 6. Finely chop the pork once
it is cool, ready for filling the pastry.

Roll each pastry ball into a rectangle 10 x 6 cm/4 x 2½ inches and
then cut each in half widthways. Put a small tablespoon of filling on
one half, brush the edges with beaten egg and position the second
piece of pastry on top. Use a fork to make indentations and to tightly
seal the edges.

Place the parcels on the greased baking sheets, brush the tops with
beaten egg and sprinkle with black sesame seeds. Bake in the preheated
oven for 20–25 minutes or until golden brown. Serve warm.

PORK & CABBAGE SHUMAI

Pork and cabbage are a popular choice of filling for home cooks in China because they are protein-packed yet inexpensive ingredients. But that doesn't stop these dumplings from being ridiculously tempting. Create the flower shape by lightly squeezing the egg dough cup in the middle.

1 batch Egg Dough, see page 8
100 g/3½ oz. raw prawns/
   shrimp, peeled and
   deveined
100 g/3½ oz. lean minced/
   ground pork
60 g/1¼ cups chopped
   cabbage
1 tablespoon oyster sauce
½ tablespoon sesame oil
1 teaspoon freshly ground
   white pepper
1 tablespoon cornflour/
   cornstarch
1 teaspoon salt
toasted white sesame seeds,
   to garnish

DIPPING SAUCE
125 ml/½ cup soy sauce
2 tablespoons sesame oil
large handful of freshly
   chopped coriander/cilantro
2 spring onions/scallions,
   sliced
1 teaspoon crushed garlic
1 tablespoon grated fresh
   ginger

bamboo steamer, lined
   with non-stick baking
   parchment

MAKES 16

Prepare the egg dough following the instructions from the basic recipe on page 8. While the dough is resting, make the filling. Mince the prawns/shrimp using a sharp knife to finely chop into small pieces. Transfer to a large mixing bowl, add the rest of the filling ingredients and mix thoroughly.

Roll out the egg dough, continuing to follow the instructions from the recipe on page 8. To assemble the shumai, place a wrapper on your palm and add a small tablespoon of filling to the centre. Gather the edges of the wrapper and gently pleat so that a basket shape is formed up and around the filling, leaving the middle exposed. Lightly tap the base of the dumpling on a work surface to flatten the bottom and make sure the filling fills the nooks and crannies. Lightly squeeze the middle with your thumb and forefinger to create the classic flower shape. Repeat for the rest of the wrappers and filling.

Arrange the shumai at the bottom of the lined bamboo steamer, leaving plenty of space between each one. Cover and steam the dumplings over boiling water for 7 minutes or until cooked through.

Make the dipping sauce while the dumplings are steaming by stirring the ingredients together in a small bowl.

Remove the dumplings from the steamer using the baking parchment to assist. Serve warm sprinkled with toasted white sesame seeds and alongside the dipping sauce.

PORK & LEEK JIAOZI

Traditional jiaozi are extremely popular at holiday celebrations such as Chinese New Year. Often prepared in an assembly line by various family members, these tasty dumplings are enjoyed by children and adults alike. The folded, plump pleated shape is a nice easy one to make.

1 batch of Wheat Dough, see page 8
100 g/3½ oz. firm tofu, drained and sliced into small cubes
pinch of salt
100 g/3½ oz. minced/ ground pork
2 Chinese chive stalks, white parts removed, finely chopped
large handful of freshly chopped coriander/cilantro
1 teaspoon Sichuan pepper
1 teaspoon black pepper
2 tablespons dark soy sauce
2 tablespoons sesame oil
1 leek, finely chopped
2 button mushrooms, finely chopped
1 tablespoon sunflower oil
black vinegar, for dipping

MAKES 16

Prepare the wheat dough following the instructions from the basic recipe on page 8. While the dough is resting, begin the filling. Sprinkle the tofu slices with salt and set aside for 30 minutes before squeezing out any excess water.

In a large bowl mix the minced/ground pork with the tofu and the rest of the ingredients apart from the sunflower oil and black vinegar.

Roll out the skins, continuing to follow the instructions from the recipe on page 8. Place a small tablespoon of filling neatly into the centre of a skin. Dip your fingertips into a small dish of water and slightly moisten the edge of half the skin. Fold the skin in half over the filling. Pinch one end together and make small folds to form pleats. The end result should be a plump sealed pocket.

Tap the dumplings base-down on your work surface to finish. As you are working, set aside the finished dumplings on a floured baking sheet under a damp cloth so they do not dry out.

Heat the sunflower oil over a medium heat in a large frying pan/skillet. Lightly fry the dumplings until golden brown on the bottom. To finish off the cooking process, place the dumplings in a large pan of boiling water. Cover with a lid and poach until they float to the surface.

Serve the dumplings hot with black vinegar for dipping.

CRISPY CHICKEN WONTONS

Deep-frying these dumplings until they are crisp transforms them into an appetizing snack. When served with the dipping sauce, they go perfectly with pre-dinner drinks. Chinese black rice vinegar is available from Asian stores.

1 chicken breast fillet (approx. 140 g/5 oz.), finely minced
4 tablespoons finely chopped fresh Chinese chives
pinch of ground Sichuan pepper
1 teaspoon light soy sauce
½ teaspoon sesame oil
16 wonton wrappers
sunflower or vegetable oil, for deep frying
salt and freshly ground black pepper

DIPPING SAUCE
2 tablespoons Chinese black rice vinegar
1 teaspoon sugar
1 garlic clove, finely chopped
½ red chilli/chile, finely chopped (optional)

MAKES 16

Thoroughly mix together the minced chicken, Chinese chives, Sichuan pepper, soy sauce and sesame oil. Season well with salt and pepper.

Mix together the ingredients for the dipping sauce and set aside.

Take a wonton wrapper and place a teaspoon of the chicken mixture in the centre of the wrapper. Brush the edges with a little cold water and bring the wrapper together over the chicken to form a parcel, pressing together well to seal properly. Set aside. Repeat the process until all 16 wrappers have been filled.

Heat the oil in a large saucepan or deep-fryer until very hot. Add four of the wontons and fry for a few minutes, until golden brown on both sides, turning over halfway through to ensure even browning. Remove with a slotted spoon and drain on paper towels. Repeat the process with the remaining wontons.

Serve at once with the dipping sauce.

SHRIMP & MANGO WONTONS

Deep-fried golden crispy wontons are a moreish pleasure to eat. The tropical mango dipping sauce provides a sweet and sharp tang to cut through the savouriness of the skin. Folding in this rustic way is simple to do but the finish is very effective.

350 g/12½ oz. raw prawns/
   shrimp, peeled and
   deveined
1 teaspoon salt
1 teaspoon freshly ground
   black pepper
small handful of freshly
   chopped coriander/cilantro
50 g/1¾ oz. firm tofu, drained
   and sliced, excess water
   pressed out
16 wonton wrappers
sunflower oil, for deep-frying

DIPPING SAUCE
4 tablepoons mayonnaise
2 teaspoons condensed milk
¼ small mango, diced into
   small cubes

MAKES 16

Use a pestle and mortar to mince the prawns/shrimp to a fine paste. Season with the salt and pepper and mix in the coriander/cilantro. Mash the tofu with a fork and add to the paste, stirring in well.

Hold a wonton skin on the palm of your hand and add a heaped teaspoon of filling to the centre. Dab the edges of the skin with a tiny bit of water and gather and scrunch the sides together in a rustic fashion. Repeat until all the filling and skins are used.

Heat the oil in a deep-fryer or large pan until it reaches 180°C/350°F. Cook the wontons in the hot oil in small batches for around a minute on either side. The wontons are cooked when they float up and the skins have turned golden brown. Drain the excess oil on paper towels.

To make dipping sauce, sweeten the mayonnaise with the condensed milk and stir in the diced mango. Serve the wontons hot with the mango dipping sauce.

FRITTERS, FRYS & PANCAKES

JAPANESE OKONOMIYAKI PANCAKES

These chunky cabbage-based pancakes are a great dinner party dish to make with friends, frying them up one at a time and adding different toppings. Originally from Osaka, the name means 'grill as you like it', so you really can make it your own. Omit the prawns/shrimp for a vegetarian option.

100 g/¾ cup white spelt flour
¼ teaspoon baking powder
½ teaspoon sea salt
150 ml/⅔ cup instant dashi, or fish or vegetable stock
2 eggs
300 g/10 oz. cabbage, thinly sliced
3 spring onions/scallions, finely chopped diagonally, reserve some for garnish
2 tablespoons vegetable oil
100 g/3½ oz. raw prawns/ shrimp, peeled and deveined
2 tablespoons kewpie (Japanese mayonnaise, see tip right), or normal mayonnaise
2 tablespoons Okonomiyaki sauce (see tip, right)
2 tablespoons bonito flakes – (dried, smoked tuna flakes, see right)
1 tablespoon pickled sushi ginger

frying pan/skillet with a fitted lid

MAKES 2

In a large bowl combine the flour, baking powder and salt. Whisk in the dashi (or fish or vegetable stock) and eggs. Then add the cabbage and most of the spring onions/scallions and combine together.

In the non-stick frying pan/skillet add a tablespoon of the vegetable oil and heat over a medium-high heat. Add half the batter in a neat round shape about 15 cm/6 inches in diameter; don't flatten it out, as Okonomiyaki should be thick. Place half the prawns/shrimp on top so they sit into the batter, cover the pan with the fitted lid and cook for about 3–4 minutes until the bottom is set and golden. Carefully turn over, place the lid back on and cook for a further 3–4 minutes until the prawns/shrimp are cooked through and the surface is golden. Turn over one last time and cook for a further 2 minutes with the lid off.

Slide the pancake onto a plate, then drizzle over half of the kewpie or mayonnaise and the Okonomiyaki sauce, top with the bonito flakes and remaining spring onions/scallions. Serve immediately with the pickled ginger on the side. Repeat for the second pancake.

TIP: You can buy Okonomiyaki sauce (as well as kewpie mayonnaise, dashi stock and bonito flakes) in an Asian market, or online. You can make your own less sugary version of Okonomiyaki sauce at home by mixing 1 tablespoon of soy sauce with 1 teaspoon of rice vinegar. It will be too thin to drizzle on top, so serve it as a dipping sauce on the side.

VIETNAMESE SHRIMP-STUFFED CRÊPES
with nuoc cham dipping sauce

**Bánh xèo is a street-food favourite of many Vietnamese when the sun sets –
it is a light savoury crêpe served with an abundance of salad leaves and herbs.**

NUOC CHAM DIPPING SAUCE
2 garlic cloves, finely chopped
2 Bird's Eye chillies/chiles,
   very finely chopped
2 tablespoons rice wine
   vinegar
1 tablespoon fresh lime juice
3 tablespoons fish sauce
   (see tip, right)
2 tablespoons maple syrup
110 ml/scant ½ cup water

PANCAKES
220 g/1¾ cups rice flour
1 tablespoon cornflour/
   cornstarch
1 teaspoon ground turmeric
1 teaspoon coconut palm
   sugar
400-ml/14-oz. can coconut
   milk
300 ml/1¼ cups cold water
vegetable oil, for frying
200 g/2 cups beansprouts
250–300 g/8–10 oz. cooked
   prawns/shrimp
sea salt and black pepper

TO SERVE
large lettuce leaves
fresh mint leaves
handful of spring onions/
   scallions, sliced

*22–24-cm/8½–9½-inch
   non-stick frying pan/skillet*

MAKES 8

For the nuoc cham sauce, combine the garlic, chillies/chiles, rice wine vinegar and lime juice in a small bowl and leave for 5 minutes. Add the rest of the ingredients, mix well and leave to one side.

To make the pancake batter, sift both flours and turmeric into a large bowl. Stir in the sugar and a pinch of salt and pepper. Slowly whisk in the coconut milk and water, ensuring there are no lumps.

Place the frying pan/skillet over a high heat. Add a little vegetable oil, and once smoking hot, ladle in a thin layer of the batter, swirling around to evenly cover the base of the pan. Turn the heat down to medium-high and fry for 3 minutes, then add some beansprouts and prawns/shrimp and cook for a further 2 minutes. The bottom of the pancake should be crisp and golden. When it is, fold over the pancake and slide it off onto a plate and serve immediately. They are best when just cooked, so serve them immediately one at a time. Start cooking another one when you are nearly finished eating the first.

To eat, place a good chunk of the pancake, some mint and slices of spring onions/scallions in a lettuce leaf, wrap it up tightly and dunk in the dipping sauce with each bite.

TIP: For the 'nuoc cham', use a good-quality Vietnamese fish sauce. Look out for the word 'nhi' on the label, which means the liquid has come from the first extraction from the fish.

COURGETTE/ZUCCHINI ONION BHAJIS
with sumac yogurt & pomegranate molasses

This stellar Middle Eastern twist on the classic Indian dish is the perfect way to use up those few extra courgettes/zucchini that you might have leftover.

SUMAC YOGURT
250 g/1 cup soy or Greek yogurt
1 tablespoon pure maple syrup
1 teaspoon sumac
sea salt

BHAJIS
450 g/1 lb. courgette/zucchini, coarsely grated
70 g/½ cup chickpea/gram flour
40 g/⅓ cup rice flour
80–100 ml/5–6 tablespoons of water
2.5-cm/1-inch piece of fresh ginger, peeled and finely grated
2 garlic cloves, peeled and crushed
1 teaspoon ground coriander
½ teaspoon cumin seeds
½ teaspoon fennel seeds
½ teaspoon mustard seeds
1 large or 2 small red onion(s), thinly sliced
small handful freshly chopped coriander/cilantro, plus extra to serve
vegetable oil, for frying
2 tablespoons pomegranate molasses, to serve

SERVES 4-6

First, make the sumac yogurt. In a bowl combine together the yogurt, pure maple syrup, sumac and a pinch of salt and set aside.

Place the grated courgette/zucchini in a sieve/strainer and press firmly to remove as much liquid as possible, then wrap in a clean dish towel and press firmly again to dry them off.

Place the flours into a large bowl and whisk in the water to create a thick batter the consistency of double/ heavy cream. Add in the ginger, garlic, spices, onion, set-aside courgette/zucchini, 1 teaspoon sea salt, most of the fresh coriander/cilantro and combine very well.

Pour 2.5 cm/1 inch of vegetable oil into a frying pan/skillet and set over a medium–high heat. If you have a cooking thermometer, it should be 180°C (350°F), if not test that the heat is right by dropping in a tiny amount of batter – if it turns golden and crisp after about 40 seconds it's ready. Carefully place separate heaped tablespoons of the mixture into the hot oil, shaping into circular mounds. Do not overcrowd the pan as it will bring the temperature of the oil down. Fry, turning once or twice until crisp and golden. Remove and drain on paper towels. Keep the cooked bhajis warm in a low oven while you fry the rest.

Serve immediately with the extra coriander/cilantro sprinkled on top. Dollop the sumac yogurt and pomegranate molasses generously over each crispy bite.

CHINESE TURNIP CAKE

In China, turnip cake is made in big batches, brought round on a trolley and fried at the dinner table until caramelized and golden. Omit the sausage for a pescatarian version of the dish.

1 Chinese turnip, peeled and grated (carrot or pumpkin will also work)
4 tablespoons sunflower oil
50 g/2 oz. raw prawns/shrimp, peeled, deveined and coarsely chopped
5 shiitake mushrooms, sliced
1 Chinese sausage, sliced
1 spring onion/scallion, sliced
127g/1 cup rice flour
1 tablespoon cornflour/cornstarch
1 teaspoon salt
1 teaspoon superfine/caster sugar
1 teaspoon ground white pepper

DIPPING SAUCE
2 tablespoons oyster sauce
1 tablespoon sesame oil

450-g/1-lb. loaf pan, lined with non-stick baking parchment

steamer large enough to hold your pan

MAKES 1 LOAF

Simmer the grated turnip in 250 ml/1 cup water for 10 minutes until softened. Keep stirring while simmering and leave the pan uncovered so that the liquid gradually reduces by half. Set aside to cool.

Heat 2 tablespoons of the oil in a large frying pan/skillet over medium heat. Add the chopped prawns/shrimp, mushrooms and sausage and stir-fry for 5 minutes. Stir in the chopped spring onion/scallion and fry for a minute longer. Let cool.

Combine the rice flour, cornflour/cornstarch, salt, sugar, and pepper in a large mixing bowl. Add the cooked turnips with their liquid and mix well. Lastly, stir in the cooked prawns/shrimp, mushrooms and sausage.

Pour the cake batter into the lined loaf pan. Place the pan into a steamer with plenty of water and steam over medium-high heat for 50 minutes. Cool the turnip cake for 10 minutes before removing from the cake pan.

Use a sharp knife dipped in water to slice 3-cm/1-inch thick pieces. Add the remaining oil to a non-stick cast iron pan/skillet over medium-low heat. Fry the cake slices on both sides until golden and crispy.

Mix together the oyster sauce and sesame oil to form a dipping sauce and serve alongside the hot cake slices.

VIETNAMESE PORK-STUFFED CRÊPES

Oriental food is often naturally healthy, yet full of flavour. This Vietnamese pancake is a perfect example, made with rice flour and coconut milk. For a pescetarian version, try the recipe on page 55.

DIPPING SAUCE
2 garlic cloves, finely chopped
2 Bird's Eye chillies/chiles, finely chopped
2 tablespoons cider vinegar
5 tablespoons fish sauce
3 tablespoons sugar

CRÊPES
200 g/1½ cups rice flour
2 teaspoons ground turmeric
400 ml/1½ cups coconut milk
2 spring onions/scallions, thinly sliced
pinch of sea salt
pinch of sugar
cooking oil, for frying
4 shallots, chopped
400 g/14 oz. pork belly, thinly sliced
200 g/7 oz. raw king prawns/jumbo shrimp, peeled and deveined (optional)
200 g/3½ cups beansprouts
sea salt and black pepper

TO SERVE
lettuce leaves
spring onions/scallions, cut into short lengths
coriander/cilantro
Thai sweet basil garden or hot mint

20-cm/8-inch non-stick frying pan/skillet with a lid

MAKES ABOUT 12

To make the dipping sauce, mix together the garlic, chillies/chiles and vinegar in a bowl. Set aside for 2 minutes. This 'cooks' the garlic. Now add the fish sauce, sugar and 400 ml/1½ cups water.

For the crêpes, mix together the flour, turmeric, coconut milk, 400 ml/1½ cups water, spring onions/scallions, salt and sugar in a bowl, making sure it is smooth and free of lumps.

Heat 1 teaspoon oil in the frying pan/skillet over medium heat and fry 1 teaspoon of the chopped shallots until browned. Season the pork belly and prawns/shrimp (if using) with salt and pepper and add a few pieces to the pan until cooked through. Using a shallow ladle, pour in a thin layer of the crêpe batter, add a handful of beansprouts and cover the pan with the lid. Allow to cook for 2 minutes. Remove the lid and cook for a further minute, making sure the crêpe is crispy and brown. Fold the crêpe in half and set aside. Repeat this whole process with the remaining shallots, batter and other ingredients to make several more crêpes.

To eat, put a piece of crêpe onto a lettuce leaf, add the onions/scallions and herbs, roll it all up and dip it in the dipping sauce.

KOREAN KIMCHI PANCAKE
with black garlic crème fraîche

This popular Korean dish contrasts the chewy-textured, chilli/chile-hot pancake with the subtle coolness of crème fraîche, enriched with the mellow sweetness of black garlic. Kimchi is a traditional Korean fermented relish, usually made with cabbage.

100 g/¾ cup plain/
　all-purpose flour
½ teaspoon salt
100 ml/⅓ cup water
3 tablespoons kimchi liquid
　(reserved from kimchi)
130 g/1 cup kimchi,
　finely chopped
1 spring onion/scallion,
　finely chopped
150 ml/⅔ cup crème fraîche
　or sour cream
3 black garlic cloves,
　finely chopped
1 tablespoon sunflower
　or vegetable oil
thinly sliced spring onion/
　scallion, to garnish

SERVES 4

Make the batter by whisking together the flour, salt and water into a thick paste. Stir in the kimchi liquid, then mix in the kimchi and spring onion/scallion.

Mix together the crème fraîche and black garlic and set aside.

Heat a large frying pan/skillet until hot. Add the oil and heat well. Pour in the batter, which should sizzle as it hits the pan, spreading it to form an even layer. Fry for 3–5 minutes until set, then turn over and fry the pancake for a further 3–4 minutes until it is well browned on both sides.

Cut the kimchi pancake into bite-size portions and serve topped with the black garlic crème fraîche. Sprinkle with extra spring onions/scallions to garnish.

OOTHAPAM Indian vegetable pancakes

Oothapam is a thick pancake made with semolina flour. The fermented version looks a bit like a crumpet, with fresh vegetables dropped into the batter as it cooks. The traditional recipe is fermented for hours, but there is also a quick version which doesn't come out as thick but is equally delicious.

vegetable oil, for frying
1–2 green chillies/chiles, to taste, thinly sliced
3 fresh or dried curry leaves, chopped
1 red onion, thinly sliced
2 tomatoes, finely chopped
1 carrot, grated
small handful of chopped kale
coconut chutney or spicy sambar chilli/chile paste, to serve

TRADITIONAL BATTER
300 g/1⅔ cups basmati rice, rinsed until the water runs clear, then drained
100 g/generous ½ cup hulled whole urid dal
½ teaspoon fenugreek seeds
½ teaspoon salt

QUICK BATTER
300 g/2 cups coarse semolina flour
300 g/1⅓ cups plain or soy yogurt
1 teaspoon freshly squeezed lemon juice
1 teaspoon bicarbonate of soda/baking soda
1 teaspoon salt
pinch of asafoetida powder (hing)

MAKES 10-14

For the traditional fermented batter, put the rice in one bowl and the dal and fenugreek seeds in another bowl, and add water to cover both by at least 5 cm/2 inches. Soak for at least 6 hours or overnight.

Drain the rice and dal mixtures, reserving both the drained liquids. Put the rice in a food processor or blender and blitz until smooth, adding about 6–7 tablespoons of the soaking water, or more if needed. Repeat with the dal mixture, adding 5 tablespoons of the soaking water and blending until smooth.

Put both mixtures in a large bowl. Mix together with the salt and cover with clingfilm/plastic wrap. Leave overnight in a warm place to ferment. The batter will keep for up to 1 week in the fridge once it is fermented, or can be frozen for up to six months.

For the quick batter, mix all the ingredients together with enough water to make a thick pouring consistency. Set aside for 10–15 minutes.

If using the fermented batter, add a little more water as necessary to make a thick pouring consistency. Add ½ tablespoon oil to a large non-stick frying pan/skillet over medium heat. Using a ladle, spoon the batter into the centre of the pan and use the back of the ladle to smooth it out to the edges. Add a little oil around the edge to ensure it doesn't stick.

Quickly remove the pan from the heat and scatter the top of the pancake with some of the prepared vegetable topping ingredients. Use the back of the ladle to push the vegetables slightly into the batter. Return the pan to the heat and cook for 3 minutes or until the pancake begins to brown underneath, then turn it over and cook for another 1–2 minutes. Repeat to make the remaining pancakes. Serve immediately with the suggested accompaniments.

INDIAN LENTIL & RICE DOSAS

The preparation for these classic Indian pancakes needs to start 36 hours in advance. A veggie curry is a good filling, but you can customize as you like.

350 g/1¾ cups basmati rice, rinsed and drained
125 g/⅔ cup white urid dal, rinsed and drained
1 teaspoon fenugreek seeds
spring or bottled water
1–2 teaspoons salt
vegetable oil, for frying
potato and pea curry, to serve
fresh coriander/cilantro and mint chutney, to serve

MAKES ABOUT 12

Put the rice and dal in separate bowls, adding the fenugreek seeds to the dal. Cover each with spring or bottled water by 5 cm/2 inches and leave to soak for 8 hours. After soaking, drain the dal, retaining the soaking water, and grind the dal and fenugreek in a food processor to a fine paste. Add 100 ml/⅓ cup of the soaking water to the paste and blend again, to achieve a smooth batter. Pour into a large bowl.

Repeat the process with the rice, grinding to a fine grainy texture, then add 125 ml/½ cup of the soaking water and blend again. Pour the rice batter into the bowl with the dal and mix thoroughly. Mix in another 250 ml/1 cup of water. The batter should coat the back of a spoon when dipped in. Cover the bowl with clingfilm/plastic wrap and set aside in a warm place to ferment for 24 hours.

When ready to make the pancakes, stir the batter, which will be frothy by now, and add the salt. It may be necessary to add more water, but make a trial pancake first. Heat a non-stick frying pan/skillet or pancake pan until medium-hot and brush with oil. Wipe off the excess oil with a paper towel. Pour a ladleful of batter onto the centre of the pan, then quickly spread it as thinly as possible, using the back of the ladle, moving it around in a spiral, starting at the centre of the pan. This has to be done quite quickly, before the batter starts to cook. The pancakes should be at least 20 cm/8 inches in diameter – if the batter doesn't spread that far, add a little more water to the bowl.

When the edges start to look lacy and crisp, lift the edge of the pancake to see if it is golden brown underneath. At this stage a little extra oil can be drizzled round the edge of the pan. Using a spatula, turn over the dosa and cook on the other side for a few minutes. Keep the pancakes warm on a plate covered with kitchen foil as you make them.

Serve each one with a spoonful of potato and pea curry spread across the centre. Spoon some fresh coriander/cilantro and mint chutney on top, and fold the pancake over from either side to seal.

KOREAN MOONG PANCAKES with pork

These savoury pancakes often contain kimchi, the Korean spiced pickled cabbage that is becoming increasingly popular around the world, but this version uses green beans instead. Either way, they make a delicious light bite.

400 g/2 cups dried moong dal (skinned and split mung beans), soaked overnight
400 ml/1⅔ cups of water
2 tablespoons soy sauce, plus extra to serve
4 garlic cloves, crushed
1 tablespoon grated fresh ginger
4 tablespoons vegetable oil
250 g/8 oz. minced/ground lean pork
1 teaspoon salt
1 leek, trimmed and finely chopped
125 g/4 oz. green beans, fresh or frozen, chopped into small pieces
chopped pickled cucumber and sliced red chilli/chile (optional), to serve

MAKES ABOUT 12

Drain the moong dal and put them in the food processor. Blend them finely, then add the water, soy sauce, all but 1 crushed garlic clove and all but ½ teaspoon of the grated ginger. Process the mixture to a smooth purée. Transfer the moong dal purée to a bowl, then leave the batter to sit for at least 30 minutes.

Meanwhile, heat 2 tablespoons of the oil in a frying pan/skillet or wok and fry the remaining garlic for 1 minute before adding the pork, together with the remaining ½ teaspoon of grated ginger and salt. Stir well and continue to cook until the pork is cooked through, then add the chopped leek and green beans and continue to cook gently until the vegetables are al dente. Take off the heat and set aside.

Heat a teaspoon of oil in a non-stick frying pan/skillet over a medium heat, and when it is hot, pour a spoonful of the batter into the pan. Spread out the batter with the back of the ladle until it forms a 8-cm/3-inch circle. Repeat the process with more batter, frying several pancakes at a time.

Cook the pancakes until golden brown on the underside and until tiny holes have begun to appear on the upper surface, then flip them over and cook the other side. This will probably take around 5 minutes on each side. It is important not to overheat the pan and burn the surface before the inside is cooked, but it must be hot enough for the pancakes to brown and crisp.

Keep warm while you make the other pancakes in the same way, brushing the frying pan or wok with oil before cooking each batch. Serve straight away with a bowl of soy sauce for dipping, and pickled cucumber and some sliced red chilli/chile, if desired.

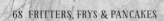

GREEN CHILLI/CHILE BHAJIS

These exotic and tasty bhajis are wonderfully adaptable. Substituting the mild green chillies/chiles for deseeded and shredded green Habaneros makes a bhaji with an intense heat that will live long in anyone's memory!

500 ml/2 cups sunflower oil
4 tablespoons coriander seeds
4 tablespoons nigella (black onion) seeds
4 tablespoons yellow mustard seeds
4 tablespoons fenugreek seeds
1 tablespoon fennel seeds
½ teaspoon whole cloves
1 large onion, diced
3–4 garlic cloves, finely chopped
5-cm/2-inch piece of fresh ginger, peeled and finely chopped
100 g/3½ oz. mild green chillies/chiles, finely chopped
60 g/¼ cup plain yogurt
grated zest and freshly squeezed juice of 2 limes

250 g/2 cups chickpea/gram flour
250 g/2 cups cornflour/cornstarch
250 ml/1 cup water
3 tablespoons hot curry powder (either Madras or Malay-style citrusy)
sea salt and freshly ground black pepper

CARAMELIZED LIME, MINT & YOGURT DIP
1 teaspoon groundnut/peanut oil
1 lime, quartered, plus extra lime zest, to garnish
300 g/1½ cups plain yogurt
few fresh mint leaves

cooking thermometer (optional)

MAKES ABOUT 16

To make the dip, heat the oil in a frying pan/skillet over a medium heat. Add the lime quarters and fry each cut side until the surface begins to develop a strong colour. It can be useful to push the lime onto the hot surface of the pan to speed this process – this will force out a little more of the juice, aiding the caramelization. Mix the yogurt and a pinch of black pepper in a small bowl. Squeeze the juice from the caramelized limes into the bowl. Take half the mint leaves and roughly tear them, then add to the bowl, too. Stir, then garnish with the rest of the mint leaves and a little lime zest. Set aside.

Put the sunflower oil in a large saucepan. Heat until it reaches 190°C (375°F) on a cooking thermometer. If you don't have a cooking thermometer, the oil is ready when a 2.5-cm/1-inch cube of white bread dropped into it browns in less than 60 seconds.

Meanwhile, toast all the seeds and the cloves in a dry frying pan/skillet over a medium heat until the seeds start to pop. Grind them using a pestle and mortar. Put the ground spices along with all the remaining dry ingredients in a bowl and mix. Gradually add the water until the mixture is firm but will drop from a spoon.

Place about 3 separate tablespoonfuls of the bhaji mix in the hot oil and fry for about 8 minutes, or until golden brown. Remove the bhajis from the pan using a slotted spoon and let drain on paper towels before serving. Continue to cook the remaining bhajis in batches and keep the already cooked bhajis warm until needed.

Serve with the caramelized lime, mint and yogurt dip.

CHINESE DUCK BREAST PANCAKES
with ginger jammy plums

You could roast and serve a whole duck if you want it crispy, but it will take a couple of hours. This recipe uses just duck breast to save time on roasting and shredding – it's juicy and easy to portion. The ginger jammy plums add flavour and look gorgeous too.

175 g/6 oz. duck breast
2 teaspoons Chinese five spice
   mixed with ½ teaspoon salt
10 ready-made Chinese
   pancakes (about 14 cm/
   5½ inches in diameter)
10 teaspoons hoisin sauce
½ cucumber, cut into
   matchsticks
5 spring onions/scallions,
   cut into matchsticks

GINGER JAMMY PLUMS
2 fresh plums, cut into
   20 wedges
freshly squeezed juice of
   1 orange
1 teaspoon grated fresh ginger
1 teaspoon caster/granulated
   sugar

MAKES 20

To make the jammy plums, simmer the plums in the orange juice, ginger and sugar for 3 minutes in a shallow frying pan/skillet until they take on a jam-like texture.

Take the duck out of the fridge 20 minutes before cooking. Score the skin of the duck and trim off any excess fat around the sides.

Rub the five spice and salt mix all over the duck. Put it in a frying pan/skillet skin-side down and turn on the heat.

When the pan is hot and you can hear the duck start to sizzle, let it cook for 5 minutes.

Sear the duck on the sides and the bottom, cooking for a further 5–8 minutes, or until cooked to your liking.

Take the pan off the heat and leave the duck to rest.

Lay the pancakes flat on a chopping board and cut in half.

Spoon ½ teaspoon hoisin sauce on a half-pancake and arrange a piece of duck, a wedge of jammy plum and a few matchsticks of cucumber and spring onions/scallions on top. Tightly roll into a flat cone. Repeat with the remaining ingredients and serve.

MUSHROOM PAKORAS

There is something irresistible about deep-fried food! These Indian pakoras – made with nutty-tasting chickpea/gram flour and flavoured with fragrant spices – are ideal for a drinks party served alongside other Indian small plates. Serve with a herbed yogurt dipping sauce or simply with lemon wedges.

115 g/¾ cup chickpea/
   gram flour
1 teaspoon ground cumin
1 teaspoon cumin seeds
½ teaspoon ground turmeric
½ teaspoon salt
½ teaspoon baking powder
120 ml/½ cup water
½ onion, chopped
200 g/6½ oz. mushrooms,
   chopped
2–3 sprigs freshly chopped
   coriander/cilantro
vegetable oil, for deep-frying
lemon wedges, to serve
   (optional)

YOGURT DIP
4 tablespoons freshly
   chopped coriander/cilantro
   or mint leaves
200 ml/1 scant cup plain
   yogurt

MAKES ABOUT 12-14

First, make the yogurt dip. Stir the chopped coriander/cilantro or mint into the yogurt and set aside.

Place the chickpea/gram flour, cumin powder and seeds, turmeric, salt and baking powder in a mixing bowl.

Whisk in the water to form a smooth batter. Fold in the onion, mushrooms and coriander/cilantro.

Heat the oil in a wok or large pan until very hot. Cook the pakoras in batches, dropping in a tablespoon of the mixture for each pakora. Fry for about 3–5 minutes, until golden brown, turning over each pakora as it cooks to ensure even browning. Remove the pakoras with a slotted spoon and drain on paper towels.

Serve at once with the yogurt dip or lemon wedges for squeezing.

AMRITSARI FISH PAKORAS

It does not get more 'Indian street food' than Amritsari fish pakoras! Deep-fried, diced cod is coated in an aromatic spiced batter, making the perfect crispy morsel. These tasty treats are traditionally found at the street-food stalls of Amritsar in Punjab, northern India, however, they are so hugely popular that they are now eaten all over the country.

500 g/1lb. 2 oz. cod loin, diced into 2.5-cm/1-inch cubes
plain/all-purpose flour, sifted, for dusting
vegetable oil, for deep-frying

MARINADE
½ green chilli/chile (or more to taste)
2 garlic cloves
1 teaspoon grated fresh ginger
2 tablespoons vegetable oil
freshly squeezed juice of ½ lemon
½ teaspoon ground turmeric
½ teaspoon salt
½ teaspoon chilli/chili powder

BATTER
4 tablespoons rice flour
8 tablespoons gram/chickpea flour, sifted

1 teaspoon ajwain seeds
1 teaspoon chilli flakes/hot red pepper flakes
1 teaspoon ground turmeric
½ teaspoon baking powder
1 tablespoon freshly chopped coriander/cilantro
180 ml/¾ cup ice-cold water
1 teaspoon salt

TO SERVE
mango powder, for sprinkling
black salt, for sprinkling
sliced chilli/chile
freshly chopped coriander/cilantro
lemon wedges

deep-fat fryer (optional)

SERVES 4-6

Rinse the diced fish under cold running water and gently pat dry.

Blitz the chilli/chile, garlic and ginger in a food processor to make a coarse paste. Combine with the rest of the ingredients for the marinade and mix with the diced fish. Let the fish pieces marinate for a minimum of 30 minutes at room temperature and a maximum of 24 hours in the refrigerator.

Combine all of the ingredients for the batter together, then set aside for 30 minutes to allow the ingredients and flavours to all come together. It should be the consistency of double/heavy cream.

Pat the marinated fish pieces in sifted flour and shake off any excess. Dip the floured fish pieces into the batter, ensuring that the fish is fully coated in the batter, with the spices distributed evenly.

Heat the oil for deep-frying in a deep-fat fryer or large, heavy-bottomed pan to 180°C (350°F). Deep-fry the fish pieces in batches of 6–8 pieces until golden-brown and the fish is cooked through; this should take no longer than 3–4 minutes per batch. Sprinkle over a pinch of mango powder and black salt, to taste, then serve with sliced chilli/chile, coriander/cilantro and lemon wedges.

SALT & PEPPER SQUID with Sansho spicy dip

This recipe, using spicy, citrusy Sansho pepper, is a spin on the ever-popular salt and pepper prawns/shrimp served in Chinese restaurants around the world. Dip the freshly fried squid into the spiced mayo and enjoy.

½ teaspoon ground
   Sansho pepper
2 teaspoons sea salt
65 g/½ cup rice flour
450 g/1 lb. squid, cleaned
   and sliced
freshly squeezed juice
   of 1 lemon
vegetable oil, for frying

SANSHO SPICY DIP
115 g/½ cup good-quality
   mayonnaise
5 g/¼ cup Vietnamese or
   regular basil leaves
½ teaspoon Sansho pepper
½ teaspoon sea salt
grated zest of 1 lemon

SERVES 4

To make the dip, whisk all the ingredients together in a small bowl until well combined. Set aside.

In a large shallow bowl mix together the Sansho pepper, salt and rice flour. Put the squid in another bowl and pour over the lemon juice.

Pour enough oil to come halfway up a large saucepan, then place over a medium–high heat until the oil starts to simmer.

Take a few pieces of squid at a time and toss in the flour mixture to coat.

Working in batches, deep fry for 2–3 minutes until golden and cooked through. Transfer to a wire rack to drain.

Pile the cooked squid in a shallow bowl and serve with the dip.

LIGHTER
BITES

VIETNAMESE SUMMER ROLLS

There are so many names for the ever-popular Vietnamese summer roll, including salad roll and crystal roll. Whatever the name, they are a fresh yet flavourful, delicious option if you are looking for an Asian bite that is not deep-fried. Here, they are stuffed with fragrant herbs and served with punchy dipping sauces which pep up the mild-tasting rice wrappers.

55 g/2 oz. rice vermicelli noodles

8 rice wrappers (21.5 cm/ 8½ inches in diameter)

4–6 shiitake mushrooms, cut into matchstick pieces

115 g/½ cup medium to firm tofu, sliced into matchstick pieces

30 g/½ cup cabbage, shredded or finely chopped

1⅓ tablespoons freshly chopped Thai basil

3 tablespoons freshly chopped mint leaves

3 tablespoons freshly chopped coriander/cilantro

2 lettuce leaves of choice, chopped

4 teaspoons fish sauce

60 ml/¼ cup water

2 tablespoons freshly squeezed lime juice

1 clove garlic, crushed

2 tablespoons caster/ granulated sugar

½ teaspoon garlic chilli/ chile sauce

3 tablespoons hoisin sauce

1 teaspoon peanuts, finely chopped

MAKES 8.

Bring a medium saucepan of water to boil. Boil the rice vermicelli for 3–5 minutes, or until al dente, and drain.

Fill a large bowl with warm water. Dip one rice wrapper into the warm water for 1 second to soften. Lay the wrapper flat. In a row across the centre of the wrapper, place 1 tablespoon of shiitake, 1 tablespoon tofu, a handful of cabbage, basil, mint, coriander/cilantro and lettuce, leaving about 5 cm/2 in. uncovered on each side. Fold the uncovered sides inward, then tightly roll the wrapper, beginning at the end with the lettuce. Repeat to make another 7 spring rolls.

In a small bowl, mix the fish sauce, water, lime juice, garlic, sugar and garlic chilli/chile sauce. In another small bowl, mix the hoisin sauce and peanuts.

Serve the spring rolls at room temperature and dip them into both sauces at will!

STEAMED ASIAN BLACK GARLIC SCALLOPS

A simple yet luxurious seafood dish, in which the natural sweetness of the scallops contrasts nicely with the savoury, smoky saltiness of the garlic dressing.

3 tablespoons dark soy sauce
2 black garlic cloves,
    finely chopped
2-cm/¾-inch piece fresh
    ginger, peeled and finely
    chopped
1 spring onion/scallion,
    finely chopped
12 king scallops
4 tablespoons groundnut/
    peanut or sunflower oil
2 black garlic cloves,
    finely chopped

steamer

SERVES 4

Mix together the soy sauce, black garlic, ginger and spring onion/scallion in a bowl and set aside.

Steam the scallops until they turn opaque and are cooked through.

Heat the oil in a small frying pan/skillet, add the garlic and fry, stirring often, until fragrant. Pour the hot garlic oil into the soy sauce mixture, mixing well to form the dressing. Spoon the garlic dressing over the freshly steamed scallops and serve at once.

VIETNAMESE CHICKEN & QUINOA BITES

The quinoa and chicken in these tasty little meatballs are both packed full of protein, making these light bites the perfect high-protein dish to serve to health-conscious dinner guests, especially after they've hit the gym.

85 g/½ cup quinoa
450 g/1 lb. minced/ground
    chicken
½ teaspoon sea salt
1 tablespoon sweet chilli/chile
    sauce, plus extra to serve
1 tablespoon cornflour/
    cornstarch
2 teaspoons sesame oil
2 tablespoons vegetable
    or coconut oil
lettuce leaves and fresh
    coriander/cilantro, to serve

SPICE PASTE
50 g/½ cup sliced shallots
20 g/½ cup fresh mint
20 g/½ cup fresh coriander/
    cilantro
2 lemongrass stalks, outer
    leaves discarded and
    roughly chopped
2.5-cm/1-inch piece fresh
    ginger
3 garlic cloves
½ tablespoon fish sauce
2 Bird's eye chillies/chiles
1 tablespoon vegetable or
    coconut oil

high-speed blender

*baking sheet, lined with
    non-stick baking parchment*

MAKES 20

Start by cooking the quinoa. Put it in a small saucepan and pour over 250 ml/1 cup of water. Set over a medium heat and bring to the boil, then reduce the heat to low. Simmer with a lid on for 10 minutes, until the quinoa is soft and fluffy and all the water has been soaked up. Leave to one side to cool down.

Preheat the oven to 200°C (400°F) Gas 6.

Add all the ingredients for the spice paste to a blender and whizz until smooth. Transfer to a large mixing bowl.

Add the ground chicken to the spice paste, then the cooled quinoa, the salt, sweet chilli/chile sauce and cornflour/cornstarch, and mix everything together.

Dampen your hands with water and roll the mixture into balls about 1 tablespoon in size. Lay the balls on the prepared baking sheet and drizzle with both the sesame and vegetable oils.

Bake in the preheated oven for 10–15 minutes, depending on the size of your balls. Once cooked, they will be white all the way through – no pink bits inside – and slightly browned on the base. Cut one open to check it is cooked all the way through.

You can eat these straight away – they are good wrapped in lettuce leaves with some fresh coriander/cilantro and sweet chilli/chile sauce on the side to dip into. You can keep them in the fridge for up to 2 days.

SMOKED DUCK SUMMER ROLLS

Called 'summer rolls' and typically served in summer months due to their refreshing nature, these can have many different fillings. This recipe uses thin slices of smoked duck breast (available from specialist food stores), but if you can't find smoked duck you could use smoked salmon or smoked trout instead.

100 g/3½ oz. rice vermicelli
    noodles
2 teaspoons fish sauce
2 teaspoons freshly squeezed
    lime juice
2 teaspoons caster/
    granulated sugar
8 x 20-cm/8-inch dried rice
    paper wrappers
100 g/3½ oz. smoked
    duck breast
100 g/3 cups thinly sliced
    lettuce
1 carrot, peeled and cut into
    thin batons
½ cucumber, deseeded and
    cut into matchsticks
20 fresh Thai basil leaves

**HOISIN & PEANUT
DIPPING SAUCE**
2 tablespoons hoisin sauce
1 tablespoon smooth peanut
    butter
1 tablespoon warm water
2 teaspoons freshly squeezed
    lime juice
1 teaspoon dark soy sauce
¼ teaspoon caster/
    granulated sugar

SERVES 4

Put the noodles in a bowl, cover with boiling water and soak for 30 minutes until softened. Drain the noodles, pat dry and transfer to a large mixing bowl. Whisk the fish sauce, lime juice and sugar together until the sugar is dissolved and pour over the noodles. Toss well and set aside.

Next make the dipping sauce. Put all the ingredients in a small saucepan set over a low heat. Heat gently, stirring until the peanut butter is softened and the sauce smooth. Remove from the heat and set aside to cool.

Working one at a time, dip the rice paper wrappers into a bowl of warm water for about a minute until softened and then pat dry on paper towels. Lay each wrapper out flat and top with a few noodles, the smoked duck slices, shredded lettuce, carrot, cucumber and basil leaves. Fold the ends of the rice paper over the filling and then roll up tightly to form parcels.

Serve with the dipping sauce.

RICE ROLLS WITH PORK & SHRIMP

Bánh cuôn are noodle sheets similar to lasagne, traditionally made from rice flour, tapioca starch and water and then steamed. They are folded or rolled, with or without a filling, and dipped into a spicy dipping sauce. They are light yet full of gorgeous flavours and textures.

FILLING
80 g/1 cup dried shredded wood ear mushrooms
dash of cooking oil
2 Asian shallots, finely chopped
300 g/10½ oz. minced/ground chicken or pork
½ teaspoon sea salt
½ teaspoon coarsely ground black pepper
2 teaspoons sugar
170 g/6 oz. king prawns/jumbo shrimp, peeled, deveined and finely chopped

NOODLE SHEETS
300 g/2¼ cups tapioca starch
300 g/2¼ cups rice flour
1 teaspoon cooking oil, plus extra for frying
2 spring onions/scallions, finely chopped
½ teaspoon salt
900 ml/scant 4 cups water

DRESSING
2 garlic cloves, finely chopped
2 Bird's Eye chillies/chiles, finely chopped
2 tablespoons cider vinegar
5 tablespoons fish sauce
3 tablespoons sugar
400 ml/1½ cups water

GARNISHES
deep-fried shallots
Thai sweet basil, finely chopped
coriander/cilantro, finely chopped

20-cm/8-inch non-stick frying pan/skillet with a lid

SERVES 6

To make the filling, put the mushrooms in a bowl, cover with warm water and soak for at least 30 minutes. Drain and pat dry.

Heat the oil in a frying pan and fry the shallots briefly. Add the meat and mushrooms and stir-fry for a couple of minutes. Add the salt, pepper, sugar and prawns/shrimp. Cook for 3 minutes, then allow to rest.

To make the noodle sheets, mix the ingredients and the water in a bowl, making sure the batter is smooth and free of lumps. Heat a dash of oil in the 20-cm/8-inch frying pan. Using a shallow ladle, pour in 1 ladleful of the batter and tilt the pan to spread the batter. Cover with the lid and cook for 2 minutes, then slide the cooked noodle sheet onto a plate. Repeat with the remaining batter.

Divide the filling between the noodle sheets. Fold the sides over the filling, then roll up tightly from the bottom. Place, seam side down, on a serving dish.

For the dressing, mix together the garlic, chillies/chiles and vinegar in a bowl. Set aside for 2 minutes. This 'cooks' the garlic. Now add the fish sauce, sugar and the water.

Serve the rolls warm or at room temperature with the garnishes and dressing sprinkled on top.

VEGAN TEMAKI ROLLS WITH SEED PÂTÉ

This hand-rolled sushi is really easy to make. Temakis are a great choice for parties since they are best rolled directly at the table, just before eating, and everybody can join in, which leaves you with less work. Prepare and serve all ingredients in the middle of the table and let the fun begin!

FERMENTED SEED PÂTÉ
240 g/2 cups pumpkin seeds
840 ml/3½ cups water, for soaking
50 ml/scant ¼ cup olive oil
60 ml/¼ cup water
1 garlic clove
¼ teaspoon turmeric powder
1 tablespoon nutritional yeast (optional)
3 teaspoons vegan rice or barley miso
2 teaspoons lemon juice
¼ teaspoon salt
freshly crushed black pepper

MAKES 250 G/2½ CUPS

TEMAKI ROLLS
2 medium carrots (around 100 g/3½ oz. total weight)
1 ripe avocado (around 190 g/6½ oz. in weight)
2 handfuls rocket/arugula or 50 g/1 cup alfalfa sprouts, plus extra to serve
3 spring onions/scallions
6 sheets of nori seaweed
2 cups Sauerkraut or other fermented vegetables, plus extra to serve
soy sauce, to serve

MAKES 12

First make the pâté. Soak the pumpkin seeds in the water for soaking for 2–3 days, until slightly fermented, without changing the soaking water. Discard the soaking water and rinse them thoroughly under running water. Drain well. Place in a high-speed blender jug/pitcher, together with the remaining ingredients. Blend until smooth, using a tamper tool to push down the ingredients. If you don't own a high-speed blender, the pâté will probably turn out chunkier in a less powerful blender, and more water will need to be added, resulting in a somewhat runnier consistency. Let sit in the fridge for another day; the flavours really develop in this final stage of setting. There will be some leftovers, but you can store these in the fridge and use within a week.

Wash and julienne the carrots. Peel the avocado, slice in half, discard the stone and cut both halves in strips. Wash the rocket/arugula or sprouts and pat dry. Take only the green parts of the spring onions/scallions, wash them well and cut into 10-cm/4-inch pieces. Cut each nori sheet in half with scissors.

Make sure your hands are dry before starting. Place a piece of nori (shiny side down) in the palm of your hand and add 1½ tablespoons of pumpkin seed pâté. Spread it gently on the left third of the nori sheet. Place your chosen fillings diagonally over the pate. Do not overfill; a couple of carrot matchsticks, 1 slice of avocado, 1 tablespoon of sauerkraut and some greens are more than enough. Fold the bottom left corner of the nori over and begin rolling into a cone shape. Wet the edge with little water and seal. Continue until all nori is used. Serve the temaki rolls with more fermented vegetables, condiments, some soy sauce and leftover greens.

SMOKED MACKEREL SUSHI ROLLS

This is a recipe for inside-out 'uramaki' rolls, which look far more difficult than they actually are! They will impress your guests.

255 g/1¼ cups brown
    or white sushi rice
550 ml/2⅓ cups water
50 ml/3 tablespoons mirin
    (sweetened rice wine)
5 sheets of nori seaweed
black sesame seeds
350 g/12 oz. smoked
    mackerel, cut into
    thin strips
2 spring onions/scallions,
    cut into thin strips
½ red (bell) pepper,
    cut into thick strips

TO SERVE
wasabi
picked Japanese sushi ginger
light soy sauce

bamboo sushi mat

SERVES 4

Wash the sushi rice under cold water and drain. Place in a saucepan with a lid and add the water. Bring to the boil (uncovered), then reduce to the lowest heat and simmer until nearly all the water has been absorbed (about 20–25 minutes). Remove from the heat, place the lid on top and allow it to stand for 15 minutes.

Spread the rice out over a clean baking sheet. Drizzle the mirin all over the rice, turning it with a spatula to help it cool down.

While it is cooling, wrap the bamboo sushi mat in clingfilm/plastic wrap, squeezing out any trapped air. This helps prevent the rice from sticking. Lay the mat lengthways in front of you. Take one nori sheet and lay it out, shiny side down, on the mat. Wet your hands and take a small handful of rice. Starting at the far end, pat the rice across the nori sheet leaving a bare ¼-cm/½-inch gap running along the edge of the sheet closest to you. Add more rice if needed, but it should be no more than 1 cm/½ inch thick.

If it starts sticking to your hands simply wet them again. You can also use the back of a spoon dipped in water.

Sprinkle black sesame seeds over the rice, then flip the nori sheet over so that the rice is facing downward with the edge free of rice closest to you and in line with the edge of the bamboo mat. Across the middle of the nori lay 3 lines of mackerel, spring onion/scallion and red pepper.

Then, using the bamboo mat, roll the edge of the nori sheet closest to you over the filling in the middle, tucking it over firmly so the filling is enclosed. When it looks like you are about to roll the mat into the sushi roll, pull the mat back and continue to roll applying even pressure and tightening as you roll, using the mat to shape it. Once the roll has come together, carefully take it off the mat, lay the mat over it and press and smooth the roll. The roll will actually be more of a rectangular shape. With a sharp and wet knife, cut the roll in half and then each half into 3.

Repeat this process with the remaining ingredients. Serve with wasabi, pickled ginger and soy sauce in a dish on the side.

SASHIMI & CUCUMBER BITES

Seasoned raw fish with flavours of ginger, soy, sesame and spring onions/
scallions, topped with avocado make a perfect Japanese-inspired light bite.
A little bit of extra chilli/chile keeps things sprightly. You can serve this
sashimi mix in lettuce cups or on cucumber slices.

600 g/1 lb. 5 oz. fresh
   or sashimi-grade fish
   (tuna is classic, but you
   can substitute any other
   sashimi-grade fish)
½ teaspoon white sugar
3 tablespoons soy sauce
1 tablespoon sesame oil
1 tablespoon grated fresh
   ginger
1 tablespoon finely chopped
   red chilli/chile
35 g/½ cup (about 5) chopped
   spring onions/scallions
1 tablespoon black sesame
   seeds, plus extra to garnish
1 tablespoon white sesame
   seeds, plus extra to garnish
1 large avocado, peeled, pitted
   and diced into 1-cm/½-inch
   dice
1 head iceberg lettuce, or thick
   cucumber slices, slightly
   hollowed out, to serve

SERVES 6-8

Trim any sinew or bloodlines off the fish. Cut the flesh into
1-cm/¾-inch dice.

Stir the sugar into the soy sauce until it dissolves.

Mix with the sesame oil, ginger and chilli/chile. Combine the soy
dressing with the fish. Gently fold through the spring onions/scallions,
sesame seeds and avocado.

Serve with lettuce leaves to wrap around or pile onto thick slices of
cucumber. Garnish with extra sesame seeds if you like.

MUSHROOM-FILLED LETTUCE CUPS

Light and elegant, with pleasantly contrasting textures, these filled lettuce leaves make an appealing light bite. Fresh oyster or shiitake mushrooms would work well in this Chinese-inspired dish. Similarly, radicchio or chicory leaves, with their distinctive bitter note, could be used instead of lettuce leaves.

1 tablespoon vegetable oil
1-cm/½-inch piece fresh
    ginger, finely chopped
1 garlic clove, finely chopped
2 spring onions/scallions,
    finely chopped, separated
    into white and green parts
300 g/10 oz. white/cup
    mushrooms, cut into
    1-cm/½-inch dice
1 tablespoon rice wine
    or Amontillado sherry
2 teaspoons light soy sauce
1 tablespoon oyster sauce
8 even-sized Little Gem
    lettuce leaves
coriander/cilantro sprigs,
    to garnish
finely chopped red chilli/
    chile, to garnish

MAKES 8

Heat the oil in a wok or large frying pan/skillet. Add the ginger, garlic and white spring onion/scallion pieces and stir-fry over a medium heat for 1 minute.

Add the diced mushrooms and stir-fry for 2 minutes. Add the rice wine or sherry and stir-fry for 1 minute, until cooked off. Add the soy sauce and oyster sauce. Stir-fry for 2 minutes. Toss through the green spring onion/scallion pieces.

While the mushroom mixture is hot or at room temperature, spoon it into the lettuce leaves, filling each one with the mixture.

Garnish with coriander/cilantro leaves and finely chopped red chilli/chile and serve at once.

TEMPURA VEGETABLES & SHRIMP
with wasabi mayonnaise

Tempura vegetables and shrimp are always a hit. This lighter, wheat-free version is made using rice and cornflour/cornstarch to give a thin crispy coating of batter to the fresh ingredients.

selection of vegetables, eg. carrot, sweet potato, aubergine/eggplant, squash, broccoli, (bell) pepper, spring onion/ scallion, beet(root)

600 ml/2½ cups vegetable, sunflower or rapeseed oil

4 king prawns/jumbo shrimp, peeled and deveined, but tails on

100 g/¾ cup rice flour, plus extra for coating

100 g/¾ cup cornflour/ cornstarch

1 teaspoon baking powder

small bottle of ice-cold sparkling water

2 egg whites

few cubes of ice

sea salt and freshly ground black pepper

5 tablespoons mayonnaise mixed with wasabi powder or paste to taste for dipping

SERVES 4

Cut the hard vegetables into thin slices about ½ cm/¼ inch thick. Cut softer vegetables like aubergine/eggplant, spring onion/scallion or (bell) pepper a little thicker.

If you have a deep fat fryer, heat the oil to 190°C/375°F, otherwise heat it in a deep saucepan. If you don't have a cooking thermometer, check the temperature by dropping a small cube of bread into the oil. It should turn golden in about 25–30 seconds. Any faster than this and the tempura will burn before the vegetable inside is cooked through.

While the oil is heating, mix together the flours, baking powder, ½ teaspoon salt and a good pinch of pepper in a bowl. Slowly stir in just enough cold sparkling water until you have a yogurt-like consistency, but don't over-whisk. It doesn't matter if the batter is lumpy; traditionally Japanese tempura batter is not mixed too thoroughly, as the lumps in the batter help to form a more crunchy tempura. Using an electric whisk, beat the egg whites in a separate bowl until they form hard peaks. Fold the eggs into the batter, stir the ice cubes through to keep it as cold as possible.

Lightly coat the vegetables and prawns/shrimp in rice flour. Shake off any excess, then dip into the batter. Carefully place them into the hot oil. Don't overcrowd the fryer or pan, as it will bring down the temperature of the oil. The prawns/shrimp will take about 3 minutes and the vegetables about 2 minutes. Remove all the tempura with a slotted spoon and drain on paper towels. Serve with the wasabi mayonnaise on the side for dipping.

SWEET-&-SOUR POPCORN TOFU

This is a Chinese-inspired fusion-style dish with healthy tofu at its core and fresh plums used to make a dipping sauce. There are quite a lot of processes involved to give the tofu perfect texture and flavour, but you can save time by using a ready-made plum sauce, if you like. For an impressive and fun way of serving, put a little sauce in a Chinese soup spoon and top with a piece of crispy tofu.

6 tablespoons light
  soy sauce
2 teaspoons Chinese
  five-spice powder
400 g/14 oz. firm
  tofu, drained,
  excess water
  pressed out and
  sliced into small
  cubes
150 g/1 cups
  cornflour/
  cornstarch
100 ml/⅓ cup soya/
  soy cream
150 g/2¾ cups panko
  breadcrumbs
1 teaspoon hot
  smoked paprika
600 ml/2½ cups
  vegetable oil, for
  deep-frying

PLUM SAUCE
12 plums, stoned/
  pitted and roughly
  chopped
2 tablespoons water
4–6 tablespoons soft
  brown sugar, if
  using fresh plums
8 tablespoons rice
  vinegar, or to taste
1 tablespoon tomato
  purée/paste, or to
  taste
½ teaspoon salt

SERVES 4–6

To make the sauce, put the plums in a pan over medium heat and add the water and sugar. Bring to the boil, then simmer for 15 minutes or until the fruit is completely softened. Add the remaining sauce ingredients and bring to a simmer again, adding a little water if necessary so that the sauce is not too thick. Using a food processor or blender, blend the sauce until smooth. Check the seasoning and adjust the sugar, salt or vinegar to taste. The balance of sweet-and-sour flavours means one should not overpower the other.

Mix the soy sauce and five-spice powder in a bowl, then drizzle this marinade over the tofu pieces. Put the cornflour/cornstarch in one bowl, the soya/soy cream in another bowl and the panko breadcrumbs in a third bowl. Add the paprika to the breadcrumbs and mix well.

Heat the vegetable oil in a wok over a medium–high heat. Put a sheet of non-stick baking parchment on the work surface. Dip each piece of tofu in the cornflour/cornstarch, then in the soya/soy cream and then in the breadcrumbs, shaping it a little to form a ball. Lay each coated ball on the baking parchment as you go.

Fry the tofu in batches, until golden brown and crispy. Lift out using a slotted spoon and drain on paper towels. You can keep the tofu balls warm in a low oven, if you like, or reheat them later at 170°C (350°F) Gas 4 for 10–15 minutes. Serve with the plum sauce.

KIMCHI NOODLE DUMPLINGS
with dipping sauce

The super-healthy, super-flavoursome wonder-ingredient kimchi is the star of the show in these delicious crispy-bottomed dumplings. Traditionally kimchi is quite fiery so just one tablespoon of chilli/hot red pepper flakes is added here, which is far less than you will find in most Korean recipes. Add more if you dare!

150 g/⅔ cup minced/
   ground pork
150 g/scant 1 cup cooked
   prawns/shrimp, peeled
   and very finely chopped
100 g/4 oz. kimchi
2 teaspoons dark soy sauce
½ beaten egg
20 gyoza wrappers
4 tablespoons vegetable oil
125 ml/½ cup water to the pan

DIPPING SAUCE
2 tablespoons dark soy sauce
1 tablespoon brown rice
   vinegar
pinch of toasted sesame
   seeds
spring onions/scallions,
   thinly sliced, to serve

baking sheet, lined with
   non-stick baking parchment

SERVES 4

Put the pork, prawns/shrimp, kimchi, soy sauce and beaten egg in a large mixing bowl and mix together until evenly combined.

Working one at a time, lay the gyoza wrappers out flat and place a teaspoon of the mixture on one half of each wrapper. Dampen the edges with a little cold water, fold the wrapper over the filling and carefully press the edges together to seal.

Preheat the oven to 110°C (225°F) Gas ¼ (or the lowest heat setting).

Heat the oil in a wok or large non-stick frying pan/skillet set over a high heat. Add half the dumplings and fry for about 1 minute until the bottoms are golden. Add the water to the pan, cover and simmer for 5 minutes until the filling is heated through. Remove the lid and cook for a further 1–2 minutes until the bottoms are crispy. Transfer the dumplings to the prepared baking sheet, turn off the oven and set in the still-warm oven while you cook the remaining dumplings in the same way.

Mix together the ingredients for the dipping sauce in a small bowl. Arrange the dumplings on warmed plates and serve with the sauce, scattered with spring onions/scallions.

VEGAN MAKI & CALIFORNIA ROLLS

These two types of sushi are so easy to make at home. Maki is where the nori is on the outside of the roll, and California rolls are where the nori is on the inside.

SPREAD
65 g/½ cup dry-roasted sunflower seeds (or use 4 tablespoons tahini)
3 teaspoons umeboshi paste
1 tablespoon dark sesame oil

SUSHI
475 g/2⅔ cups cooked brown rice
2 medium pickled gherkins, cut lengthways into strips, or other pickled vegetables (sauerkraut, daikon, etc.)
1 long carrot, cut lengthways into thin sticks
4 long spring onion/scallion leaves, washed and drained
4 toasted nori sheets

DIPPING SAUCE
2 tablespoons fresh ginger juice
2 teaspoons tamari
2 tablespoons dry-roasted sesame seeds
4 tablespoons water
extra pickles and wasabi paste, to serve

sushi mat

MAKES 32

Prepare the spread by blending the sunflower seeds in a blender into a powder/butter, and then adding the umeboshi and oil.

Prepare a bowl full of lukewarm water to wet your hands with while making the sushi. Place each nori sheet in turn on a sushi mat, shiny-side down. Wet your hands and spread 120 g/¾ cup of the cooked rice evenly over the nori, except the top side, where you'll want to leave a 1-cm/⅓-in. margin to make it easier to roll and seal.

To make the maki, spread a tablespoon of the spread across the middle of the roll. Place a quarter of the gherkin strips, carrot sticks and spring onion/scallion leaves over the spread, making sure the layer is not thick, as this will make for an overly thick sushi.

Starting from the bottom, roll up the nori and tuck in the vegetables. Continue rolling and press tightly so that the rolled sushi stays sealed. Before serving, slice each sushi into 8 pieces. Repeat the process for the a second nori sheet, so you end up with 16 pieces of sushi.

To make California rolls, cover the sushi mat with a sheet of clingfilm/plastic wrap and place one nori sheet on top. Wet your hands and spread 120–150 g/¾–1 cup of the rice over the nori, distributing it evenly up to the edges. Carefully flip the nori so that the rice side goes on top of the clingfilm/plastic wrap on the mat. Spoon a tablespoon of the spread in a strip across the middle of the roll. Place half the remaining gherkin, carrot and spring onion/scallion leaves over the spread. Starting at the edge while pressing it firmly, roll up the sushi mat and continue until you reach the end of the mat. Be careful not to wrap the clingfilm/plastic wrap inside! Squeeze the sushi inside the mat with your hands. Unwrap before serving, and slice into 8 pieces. Roll each of these pieces in toasted sesame seeds. Repeat with last nori sheet and remaining vegetables.

To make the sauce, mix the ginger juice, tamari and water. Dip a piece of sushi in it. Before eating, coat in some sesame seeds (but not for the California rolls, as they won't need it!) Serve the sushi with extra pickles and, if you wish, a little wasabi paste, to spice things up!

CAULIFLOWER & KALE PAKORAS

Pakoras are easy to adapt to whichever seasonal vegetables you have available. Cauliflower and kale are a great combination because the kale adds extra crispness. You can make a big batch at home, as they keep well in the fridge and can easily be reheated in the oven. Gram flour is made from chickpeas, which is a good source of protein, it is also a naturally gluten-free recipe (although it's a good idea to check the asafoetida powder if you are serving to coeliacs/celiacs).

1 small cauliflower, cut into 2-cm/¾-inch florets
1 tablespoon sunflower oil, plus extra for deep-frying
2 onions, thinly sliced
a bunch of kale or dark leaf cabbage, thinly sliced
2–4 small green chillies/ chiles, to taste, finely chopped
2 large red chillies/chiles, finely chopped
1 tablespoon chilli/chili powder
½ teaspoon asafoetida powder (hing)
250 g/2 cups chickpea/ gram flour
2 teaspoons black cumin seeds
2 tablespoons fennel seeds
2 tablespoons dried pomegranate seeds (anardana)
bunch of fresh coriander/ cilantro, roughly chopped
¼ teaspoon bicarbonate of soda/baking soda
1 teaspoon salt
daniya or raita, to serve

MAKES ABOUT 24

Parboil the cauliflower for 2–3 minutes, then drain in a colander/ strainer and leave for 5 minutes.

Heat the oil in a small pan over medium heat and fry the onions for 5 minutes or until softened. Add the kale, green and red chillies/chiles, chilli/chili powder and asafoetida, and cook for 3 minutes. Set aside.

Sift the chickpea/gram flour into a large bowl. Toast the cumin and fennel seeds in a dry pan over medium heat for 30 seconds, stirring occasionally, to release the aroma, then add to the gram flour followed by the onion and kale mixture. Add 120 ml/scant ½ cup water to make a thick paste, then add all the other ingredients and mix well. The batter should have a thick porridge-like consistency, so add a little more gram flour or water if necessary.

Heat the oil for deep-frying in a deep pan or deep-fat fryer. Using a tablespoon, gently drop spoonfuls of the mixture into the hot oil, frying in batches of three or four. Cook until golden brown, turning halfway through to cook both sides. Remove with a slotted spoon and drain on paper towels. Serve hot, with some daniya or raita for dipping.

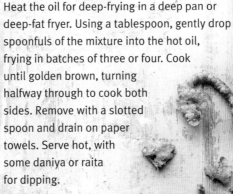
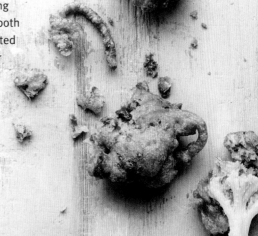

BEEF BULGOGI & RICE NOODLE WRAPS

The word bulgogi means 'fire meat' and refers to marinated and grilled meats, usually beef. Here it is stir-fried and combined with shiitake mushrooms and Korean sweet potato noodles, wrapped in lettuce leaves and topped with kimchi and ssamjang.

500 g/1 lb. beef rib-eye steak
2 tablespoons light or dark soy sauce
2 tablespoons soft brown sugar
1 Asian shallot, finely chopped
1 garlic clove, crushed
2 teaspoons sesame oil, plus extra for dressing
½ teaspoon Chinese five-spice powder
125 g/4 oz. spiralized sweet potato noodles
2 tablespoons peanut oil
125 g/4 oz. shiitake mushrooms, trimmed and cut into quarters
4 tablespoons kimchi
Ssamjang (Korean spicy sauce), to serve

SERVES 4

Begin by preparing the beef. Thinly slice the steak and arrange in a single layer in a wide, shallow dish. Combine the soy sauce, sugar, shallot, garlic, sesame oil and Chinese five-spice powder, and pour over the beef. Set aside to marinate for at least 1 hour.

Plunge the sweet potato noodles into a pan of boiling water and cook for 4–5 minutes until al dente. Drain, refresh under cold water and drain again. Shake the noodles dry and dress with a little sesame oil to prevent them from sticking together. Set aside.

Heat the oil in a wok or large frying pan/skillet set over a medium heat until it starts to shimmer. Add the beef in batches and stir-fry for 2–3 minutes until golden. Remove with a slotted spoon. Add the mushrooms and any remaining marinade and stir-fry for 1 minute. Return the beef to the pan along with the noodles and stir-fry for 1 minute, until everything is heated through.

Serve with lettuce leaves, kimchi and the ssamjang Korean spicy sauce. Wrap, roll and eat.

RIBS, GRILLS
& WINGS

KOREAN STICKY RIBS

Gochujang is a red pepper paste used in Korean cooking. It comes in varying degrees of heat, so make sure to check the label and choose something to suit your tastebuds. These ribs are great for the barbecue; serve them with an Asian coleslaw or kimchi.

8 Korean-style beef ribs,
   1 cm/½ inch thick
3 spring onions/scallions,
   finely sliced
2 tablespoons black
   sesame seeds

MARINADE
60 ml/¼ cup soy sauce
60 ml/¼ cup toasted
   sesame oil
140 g/½ cup orange-blossom
   honey
2 heaped tablespoons
   gochujang or sambal oelek
   (Asian chilli/chile paste)
1 tablespoon fish sauce
4 garlic cloves, bashed
2 Serrano chillies/chiles,
   roughly chopped
2 teaspoons cracked
   rainbow peppercorns
½ teaspoon sea salt

SERVES 4-6

Lay the ribs in a single layer in a ceramic baking dish.

Put all the marinade ingredients in a blender and process until smooth. Pour over the ribs and sprinkle with the spring onions/scallions and sesame seeds. Cover and refrigerate for 6–24 hours.

Remove the ribs from the fridge and bring to room temperature.

Heat a grill/broiler or barbecue to a medium–high heat. Place the ribs on the rack and cook for 5 minutes, then turn over and cook for another 5 minutes. Transfer to a warm plate and tent with foil. Rest for 10 minutes.

Put the remaining marinade in a small saucepan and bring to the boil, then reduce the heat and simmer for 5 minutes. To serve, pour the marinade into a bowl and serve alongside the ribs.

TANDOORI-SPICED LAMB CHOPS

The marinade for these tandoori-spiced, charred and grilled/broiled chops works exceptionally well to enhance the natural meatiness of the dish. The blend of spices, mint, chilli/chile and lemon keeps the meat moist while also creating a wonderful harmony of flavours. Lamb chops don't tend to dry out too much because they are cooked on the bone and have a layer of fat.

2 teaspoons cumin seeds
4 tablespoons plain yogurt
1 teaspoon salt
5 garlic cloves
a 5-cm/2-inch piece fresh
    ginger
4 green chillies/chiles
1 red chilli/chile
1 teaspoon ground turmeric
1 teaspoon garam masala
5 fresh mint leaves,
    plus extra to garnish
freshly squeezed juice
    of ½ lemon
12 lamb chops
vegetable oil, for frying

SERVES 6–8

Toast the cumin seeds in a dry frying pan/skillet over low–medium heat until they become dark in colour and give off a fragrant aroma. Put all of the ingredients including the toasted cumin seeds (but not the lamb chops) in a food processor and blitz until everything comes together to form a coarse chunky paste.

Rub the paste all over the lamb chops, wearing gloves if needed. Allow the chops to marinate for 24 hours in the refrigerator if possible, or for at least 30 minutes at room temperature.

Preheat the grill/broiler to high.

Heat a little oil in a frying pan/skillet over medium heat and seal the chops on both sides for 1 minute. Transfer to a baking sheet and put under the preheated grill/boiler. Grill/broil the chops for 5 minutes on each side for medium-rare. If you want them more well-done, then leave them under the grill/broiler for a little longer.

Sprinkle the chops with mint leaves and serve straight away to prevent them from drying out.

ASIAN CARAMEL WINGS

Fried first and then tossed in a sweet yet savoury caramel sauce, these wings have the perfect balance of delicate Asian flavours and seasoning. They are tastier still when served with a green onion dipping sauce on the side.

200 g/1 cup brown sugar
120 ml/½ cup water
75 ml/⅓ cup fish sauce
75 ml/⅓ cup soy sauce
60 ml/¼ cup orange juice
60 ml/¼ cup freshly squeezed
    lime juice
vegetable oil, for frying
1.8 kg/4 lbs. chicken wings,
    halved at the joints, tips
    removed

**GREEN ONION
DIPPING SAUCE**
250 ml/1 cup sour cream
225 g/1 cup mayonnaise
50 g/½ cup finely chopped
    spring onions/scallions
30 g/½ cup finely chopped
    fresh flat-leaf parsley
2 garlic cloves, finely chopped
1 teaspoon Dijon mustard

a deep fat fryer

SERVES 4-6

First, make the dipping sauce. Mix all the ingredients together in a blender until smooth. Cover and refrigerate until ready to serve.

Place the sugar in a medium saucepan with half of the water and bring to a boil. Continue to boil and swirl (don't stir) for 6–7 minutes so the sugar caramelizes evenly.

Combine the fish sauce, soy sauce, orange juice and lime juice with the remaining water in a small bowl. Once the caramel has turned a golden amber colour, slowly pour the fish sauce mixture into the pan and return to a boil. Continue to boil for 7 minutes until the sauce is well combined, then remove the sauce from the heat and keep warm.

Meanwhile, preheat the oil in the deep fat fryer to 180°C (350°F).

Fry the chicken wings in batches for about 10 minutes until cooked through and the juices run clear when the thickest part is pierced to the bone. Remove and drain on paper towels. Place in a large bowl, pour the caramel sauce over the wings and toss. Serve with the green onion dipping sauce on the side.

Serve these wings as they are for a bar bite but add rice and an Asian-style slaw to create a more substantial plateful.

THAI-STYLE FRIED CHICKEN WINGS

Let's be honest, for some fried chicken isn't so much of a craze as it is a way of life. This recipe is spicy, crispy and perfect for Friday night feasting.

vegetable or canola oil,
  for frying
9 garlic cloves
7.5-cm/3-inch piece of fresh
  ginger, peeled
6 tablespoons soy sauce
6 tablespoons curry paste
3 tablespoons rice vinegar
2 tablespoons coconut oil,
  melted
2 tablespoons runny honey
180 g/1⅓ cups plain/
  all-purpose flour
2 tablespoons cornflour/
  cornstarch
350 ml/1⅔ cups water
1.8 kg/4 lbs. chicken wings,
  halved at the joints, tips
  removed

**LEMONGRASS &
SOY DIPPING SAUCE**
3 stalks of lemongrass
2 spring onions/scallions,
  chopped
1 teaspoon finely chopped
  garlic
1 teaspoon brown sugar
1 tablespoon sriracha sauce
3 tablespoons freshly
  squeezed lime juice
1 tablespoon fish sauce
2 teaspoons soy sauce
1 tablespoon freshly chopped
  coriander/cilantro
1 tablespoon freshly chopped
  basil
3 tablespoons water

SERVES 4-6

First, make the dipping sauce. Trim the end of the lemongrass stalks and remove the outer layers, then finely chop. Place in a bowl with the other ingredients. Mix well, then cover and chill in the refrigerator until ready to serve.

Preheat the oil in the deep fat fryer to 180°C (350°F).

Chop the garlic and ginger by pulsing briefly in a food processor. Add the soy sauce, curry paste, vinegar, coconut oil and honey. Purée until smooth. Put the sauce into a bowl.

In a separate bowl, whisk the flour and cornflour/cornstarch with the water. Add the chicken and toss until well coated.

Fry the chicken in about three batches for 6–8 minutes until golden, then drain on paper towels.

Bring the oil back to 180°C (350°F) and fry the chicken for a further 6–8 minutes, until crisp and the juices run clear when the thickest part is pierced to the bone. Drain again, then toss the chicken in the sauce.

Serve with the lemongrass and soy dipping sauce.

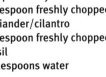

SAKE WINGS

These oven-fried, Asian-inspired chicken wings are flavoured with reduced sake, teriyaki sauce, ginger and chilli flakes/hot red pepper flakes. A teri-sake infusion!

250 ml/1 cup soy sauce

120 ml/½ cup sake, dry sherry or dry white wine

3 tablespoons very finely chopped fresh ginger

1½ tablespoons finely chopped garlic

200 g/1 cup sugar

1½ teaspoons chilli flakes/hot red pepper flakes

100 g/1 cup thinly sliced spring onions/scallions, (white and green parts), plus extra for garnish

3½ tablespoons rice vinegar

3 tablespoons cornflour/cornstarch

2 tablespoons toasted sesame seeds

1.8 kg/4 lbs. chicken wings, halved at the joints, tips removed

SERVES 4-6

PLUM DIPPING SAUCE

1.3 kg/3 lbs. plums, pitted and chopped

4 garlic cloves, finely chopped

1 tablespoon finely chopped fresh ginger

1 small onion, finely chopped

200 g/1 cup brown sugar

2 tablespoons teriyaki sauce

1 teaspoon sesame oil

2 tablespoons soy sauce

½ teaspoon crushed dried chilli

freshly squeezed juice of 1 lemon

475 ml/2 cups water

2 tablespoons cornflour/cornstarch

First, make the plum dipping sauce. Place all the ingredients except the cornflour/cornstarch in a medium saucepan with the water. Bring to the boil, then reduce the heat and simmer for 30 minutes. Remove from the heat. Mix the cornflour/cornstarch with 1 tablespoon water, then pour into a blender with the plum mixture. Blend until combined. Pour back into the pan and cook on medium-low until the mixture thickens to the desired consistency. Set aside to cool, then refrigerate until needed.

In a small saucepan, whisk together the soy sauce, sake (or sherry or white wine), ginger, garlic, sugar, chilli flakes/hot red pepper flakes, spring onions/scallions, vinegar and cornflour/cornstarch with 3 tablespoons water. Set the pan over a medium heat and bring to the boil, whisking constantly (the mixture will be very thick). Let cool.

Preheat the oven to 190°C (375°F) Gas 5. Grease 2–3 baking sheets with cooking spray or vegetable oil.

Add the sauce mixture to a large bowl with the wings and mix well. Arrange the wings in a single layer on the baking sheets and pour over any leftover sauce. Bake in the preheated oven for 30 minutes. Stir and turn the wings over in the sauce, then bake for a further 20 minutes. Stir and turn the wings again and bake for a final 10 minutes, or until the chicken is tender and the juices run clear when the thickest part is pierced to the bone, and the sauce is thick and shiny. Transfer to a serving platter. Spoon some of the extra sauce over, then sprinkle with the sesame seeds and spring onions/scallions.

VIETNAMESE BBQ SPARERIBS

This mouthwatering fusion recipe has been adapted slightly to include English mustard as an ingredient. Your guests will be crazy in love for these succulent spareribs – they will polish off every last shred of meat. This marinade can also be used for chicken thighs, drumsticks and pork chops.

4 Asian shallots, finely chopped
1 large garlic clove, finely chopped
4 teaspoons English mustard
4 teaspoons soy sauce
6 tablespoons hoisin sauce
1 tablespoon Sriracha chilli sauce
1 teaspoon honey
800 g/1¾ lbs. pork spareribs (or chicken wings, thighs, drumsticks or chops)
1 teaspoon sesame seeds (optional)

SERVES 4-6

In a bowl, mix together all the ingredients (except the meat) to make a marinade. Add the meat and rub the marinade in well. Cover and refrigerate for at least 30 minutes.

Preheat the oven to 200°C (400°F) Gas 6.

Transfer the meat to a roasting pan and roast in the preheated oven for 45 minutes or until cooked through and the juices run clear when you stick a knife in. The meat can also be grilled on a barbecue, in which case times will vary, so check that it's cooked through before serving.

Scatter the sesame seeds over the top before serving, if using.

KUNG PAO WINGS

These hot and spicy Chinese chicken wings are sautéed in a pan for tender meat and a sweet and sticky sauce. Serve with other Chinese inspired bites such as Sweet & Sour Popcorn Tofu (see page 102).

120 ml/½ cup white wine
120 ml/½ cup soy sauce
4 tablespoons sesame oil,
50 g/½ cup cornflour/
  cornstarch, dissolved
  in 120 ml/½ cup water
1.8 kg/4 lbs. chicken wings,
  halved at the joints, tips
  removed
85 g/3 oz. hot chilli paste
1½ tablespoons distilled
  white vinegar
3 tablespoons brown sugar
4 spring onions/scallions,
  chopped, plus extra to
  garnish
4 garlic cloves, finely chopped
450-g/16-oz. can water
  chestnuts, drained and
  sliced
100 g/1 cup chopped peanuts
1 fresh red chilli/chile, sliced,
  to garnish

SERVES 4-6

Combine 4 tablespoons of the wine, 4 tablespoons of the soy sauce, 2 tablespoons of the sesame oil and 4 tablespoons of the cornflour/cornstarch mixture in a bowl and mix together. Place the wings in a large, resealable plastic bag. Add the marinade, seal the bag and toss to coat. Place in the refrigerator to marinate overnight, or for at least 4 hours.

In a small bowl combine the remaining wine, soy sauce, oil and cornflour/cornstarch mixture with the chilli paste, vinegar and sugar. Mix together and add the chopped onion, garlic, water chestnuts and peanuts. Transfer the mixture to a medium frying pan/skillet and heat the sauce slowly until aromatic.

Meanwhile, remove the chicken from the marinade and sauté in a second large frying pan/skillet until the meat is cooked through and the juices run clear when the thickest part is pierced to the bone. When the sauce is aromatic, add the sautéed chicken to it and let it simmer together until the sauce thickens, then serve immediately. Garnish with the sliced chilli/chile and spring onion/scallion.

THAI GREEN CURRY WINGS

Of all the curries, Thai green curry seems to have the most flavour and aroma. Here, chicken wings are baked with a spicy green curry sauce – they are perfect for a Thai tapas feast!

vegetable oil, for greasing
2 tablespoons plain/
  all-purpose flour
2 teaspoons salt
2 teaspoons ground coriander
1.8 kg/4 lbs. chicken wings,
  halved at the joints, tips
  removed
5 tablespoons green chilli
  sauce (either hot or mild,
  depending on your taste)
4 tablespoons unsalted butter,
  melted
1 tablespoon fish sauce
2 teaspoons Thai green curry
  paste
3 tablespoons freshly
  chopped coriander/cilantro,
  to garnish
1 red chilli/chile, sliced,
  to garnish

COCONUT CREAM
DIPPING SAUCE
400-g/16-oz. can of
  coconut milk
225 g/1 cup brown sugar

SERVES 4–6

First, make the dipping sauce. Combine the ingredients in a medium saucepan and bring to the boil over a medium-high heat. Reduce the heat to medium-low and cook, stirring, for about 20 minutes until the mixture is thick and the volume has reduced by about half. Set aside until needed.

Preheat the oven to 200°C (400°F) Gas 6. Line 2–3 baking sheets with foil and grease with cooking spray or vegetable oil.

In a bowl, mix the flour with the salt and ground coriander. Add the chicken and toss to coat. Spread the chicken on the baking sheets in a single layer and sprinkle with vegetable oil.

Roast the chicken in the preheated oven for 45 minutes, turning once or twice, until browned and crispy and the juices run clear when the thickest part is pierced to the bone.

In a bowl, whisk together the chilli sauce, butter, fish sauce and curry paste. Add the cooked chicken wings to the sauce and toss. Sprinkle with the chopped coriander/cilantro and sliced chilli/chile and serve with Coconut Cream Dipping Sauce on the side.

BBQ PORK-BELLY SKEWERS

All of Sài Gòn is perfumed with smoke from honey-grilled pork at lunchtime, and bún thịt nuóng (grilled/broiled meat on noodles) is a favourite. It is a great example of Vietnamese cuisine: juicy, sweet, savoury and succulent meat with vermicelli, sharp pickles and herbs create layers of flavours and textures.

1 lemongrass stalk, finely chopped
a 5-cm/2-inch piece galangal, finely chopped (optional)
2 shallots, finely chopped
4 garlic cloves, chopped
1 tablespoon honey
2 teaspoons fish sauce
2 tablespoons vegetable oil
1 tablespoon tapioca starch
½ teaspoon black pepper
1 tablespoon sugar
1 teaspoon shrimp paste
400 g/14 oz. pork belly, cut into bite-size pieces

DIPPING SAUCE
4 tablespoons cider vinegar
4 tablespoons sugar
4 tablespoons fish sauce
2 garlic cloves, finely chopped
2 Bird's Eye chillies, finely chopped
4 tablespoons of hot water

TO SERVE
lettuce leaves
4 tablespoons roasted salted peanuts, crushed
pickled carrots and rice noodle salad (optional)

10–12 bamboo skewers, soaked in cold water for 30 minutes

SERVES 4

First, make the dipping sauce, mix all the ingredients in a bowl. Cover and refrigerate until ready to serve.

Put the lemongrass, galangal, shallots, garlic, honey, fish sauce, oil, tapioca starch, pepper, sugar and shrimp paste in a bowl. Mix well, add the pork pieces and rub the mixture into the meat. Marinate in the fridge for 20 minutes.

Preheat the oven to 180°C (350°F) Gas 4, or preheat a grill/broiler to high.

Push 3–4 pork belly pieces onto each soaked skewer. Cook in the preheated oven for about 18 minutes, or under a preheated grill/broiler for 12–15 minutes, until well browned.

Serve with lettuce leaves, a sprinkling of crushed peanuts, pickled carrots and a rice noodle salad, if liked.

THAI PEANUT CHICKEN WINGS

These moreish chicken wings are grilled/broiled for extra crispness and served with a warm peanut satay-style sauce.

4 garlic cloves, finely chopped
225 g/1 cup smooth peanut butter
120 ml/½ cup freshly squeezed lemon juice
1 tablespoon crushed chilli flakes/hot red pepper flakes, plus extra for garnish
1½ tablespoons ground cumin
250 ml/1 cup warm water
1.8 kg/4 lbs. chicken wings, halved at the joints, tips removed
sea salt flakes, to taste
fresh flat-leaf parsley, chopped
cucumber wedges, to serve

SERVES 4–6

Whisk together the garlic, peanut butter, lemon juice, crushed chilli flakes/hot red pepper flakes and ground cumin with the warm water. Season with salt.

Toss the chicken wings with 225 g/1 cup of the sauce, cover and marinate in the refrigerator overnight or for at least 2 hours.

Preheat the grill/broiler to high. Grill/broil the chicken, for 20–25 minutes, turning occasionally, until cooked through, lightly charred and the juices run clear when the thickest part is pierced to the bone.

Serve the wings with the remaining peanut sauce, topped with chopped flat-leaf parsley and crushed chilli flakes/hot red pepper flakes, accompanied by chunky cucumber wedges to counteract the spicy heat.

STICKY TERIYAKI WINGS

These oven-baked teriyaki wings are marinated in a tangy pineapple-based teriyaki sauce. Serve with green onion–ranch dipping sauce.

350 ml/1½ cups soy sauce
300 g/1½ cups sugar
175 ml/¾ cup pineapple juice
120 ml/½ cup vegetable oil
2 garlic cloves, finely chopped
1½ tablespoons finely
    chopped fresh ginger
350 ml/1½ cups water
1.8 kg/4 lbs. chicken wings,
    halved at the joints, tips
    removed

**GREEN ONION–RANCH
DIPPING SAUCE**
225 ml/1 cup sour cream
225 g/1 cup mayonnaise
35 g/½ cup finely chopped
    spring onions/scallions
1 tablespoon finely chopped
    fresh flat-leaf parsley
1 garlic clove, finely chopped
1 teaspoon Dijon mustard

SERVES 4–6

First make the dipping sauce by combining all the ingredients in a blender and whizzing until smooth. Transfer to a small bowl, cover and refrigerate until ready to serve.

Combine the soy sauce, sugar, pineapple juice, vegetable oil, garlic and ginger in a large bowl with the water. Stir until the sugar has dissolved. Pour the marinade into a large resealable plastic bag. Add the wings to the bag and marinate in the refrigerator overnight or for at least 4 hours.

Preheat the oven to 180°C (350°F) Gas 5. Line 2–3 baking sheets with foil.

Remove the chicken from the marinade and arrange on the baking sheets. Brush with the remaining marinade. Bake in the preheated oven for about 1 hour, or until the juices run clear when the thickest part is pierced to the bone.

Serve these wings with the green onion-ranch dipping sauce for a bar bite but add cooked rice noodles and wilted Chinese cabbage/pak choi for a more substantial plateful.

CHARRED SHRIMP WITH NAM JIM

This is such a simple yet effective dish and is great for diving into and getting your hands dirty with a big group of friends. The Nam Jim is a wonderfully vibrant Thai sauce that makes these totally addictive. Make sure you use the roots of the coriander/cilantro and not the leaves, as this is where all the flavour is. Healthy coconut palm sugar is used here, it has been used for hundreds of years in Southeast Asian cooking. Don't confuse it with Thai palm sugar, which comes in white hard blobs.

roots of 1 bunch of fresh coriander/cilantro plus reserved leaves for garnish
2 garlic cloves
2.5-cm/1-inch piece fresh ginger
1 large red chilli/chile, deseeded, plus extra slices for garnish
1 tablespoon coconut palm sugar
sea salt
2 teaspoons fish sauce
freshly squeezed juice of 1 lime
8 raw king prawns/jumbo shrimp, shell on

ridged stovetop griddle pan/ grill pan

SERVES 3-4

Using a pestle and mortar, pound the coriander/cilantro roots, garlic, ginger and chilli/chile until you get a paste. This will take a few minutes of fairly aggressive pounding! The skin of the chilli/chile will also come loose so when that happens, you should pick it out and discard it.

Add the sugar and pound, then add a little salt, the fish sauce and lime juice. Mix together and taste. Adjust it ever so slightly until you get the right balance.

Heat a stovetop griddle pan/grill pan over a high heat. Cut the prawns/ shrimp lengthways down the middle of the belly, so you have long halves. Place them, flesh-side down, on the dry pan, cook for 2 minutes, then flip them over and cook for another 2 minutes.

Once cooked, arrange the prawns/ shrimp together on a plate scattered with the reserved coriander/cilantro leaves and extra chilli/chile slices. Drizzle with Nam Jim and serve.

SPICY PORK SATAY SKEWERS
with peanut sauce

These spicy pork skewers dipped in peanut sauce are heaven on a stick. They are great for weekend get-togethers, when you want to make delicious, easy food with minimum kitchen time. You can also pop these on a barbecue and forgo the hob.

450 g/1 lb. pork tenderloin
coriander/cilantro leaves and lime wedges, to garnish

SPICY MARINADE
2 tablespoons rice wine vinegar
2 green chillies/ chiles, chopped
1 tablespoon soy sauce
1 large garlic clove, finely chopped
1 tablespoon toasted sesame oil
2 tablespoons fish sauce
2 tablespoons peanut/groundnut oil
2 tablespoons freshly chopped coriander/ cilantro leaves
1 tablespoon grated fresh ginger

PEANUT SAUCE
1 tablespoon peanut/ groundnut oil
1 garlic clove, finely chopped

2 red Thai chillies/ chiles, finely chopped
4 kaffir lime leaves
1 stalk lemongrass, cut into 4
1 teaspoon garam masala or curry powder
2 tablespoons dark brown sugar
225 g/1 cup peanut butter
250 ml/generous 1 cup coconut milk
30 g/⅓ cup unsweetened coconut flakes
finely grated zest and freshly squeezed juice of 1 lime
2 tablespoons fish sauce

18–20 short metal skewers

ridged stovetop griddle pan/grill pan

MAKES 18–20 SKEWERS

Slice the pork into ½-cm/1/4-inch thick pieces and put in a bowl. Mix together all the Spicy Marinade ingredients and pour over the pork. Cover and put in the refrigerator for 30 minutes.

To make the peanut sauce, heat the peanut oil in a saucepan over medium heat. Sauté the garlic, chillies/ chiles, kaffir lime leaves, lemongrass and garam masala for 2 minutes. Add the sugar and stir. Now add the peanut butter, coconut milk and coconut flakes, along with the lime zest and juice. Cook for 15 minutes. Take off the heat and stir in the fish sauce. Pour the mixture into a bowl and set aside.

Remove the pork from the refrigerator and thread onto the skewers.

Heat the griddle pan/grill pan over high heat until nearly smoking. Grill the pork skewers for 3–4 minutes each side until brown and caramelized.

Garnish the pork skewers with coriander/cilantro leaves and serve with lime wedges and the peanut sauce on the side.

YAKITORI-GLAZED MUSHROOM & CHICKEN SKEWERS

These salty-sweet glazed chicken skewers go down well with all the family! Fresh shiitake mushrooms, with their distinctive flavour, are a pleasing element in the dish.

16 white/cup mushrooms, stalks trimmed off
250 g/8 oz. boneless chicken breast, cut into short, thin strips
16 fresh shiitake mushrooms, halved, stalks trimmed off
½ green (bell) pepper, deseeded and cut into 2-cm/1-inch squares
2 spring onions/scallions, cut into 2-cm/¾-inch lengths
finely sliced red chilli/chile, to garnish (optional)

YAKITORI GLAZE
50 ml/3 tablespoons rice wine or Amontillado sherry
50 ml/3 tablespoons mirin
50 ml/3 tablespoons light soy sauce
1 tablespoon white granulated sugar
¼ teaspoon salt

8 long metal skewers

SERVES 4-6

Make the yakitori glaze by placing the rice wine or sherry, mirin, soy sauce, sugar and salt in a small saucepan. Bring to the boil and boil for 1 minute until melted together into a syrupy glaze. Turn off the heat.

Thread the white/cup mushrooms, chicken, shiitake mushrooms, green (bell) pepper and spring onions/scallions onto the skewers.

Preheat the grill/broiler to high. Brush the prepared skewers generously with the yakitori glaze. Grill/broil the skewers for 8–10 minutes, until the chicken is cooked through, brushing repeatedly with the glaze and turning the skewers over halfway through.

Sprinkle with some finely sliced chilli/chile if liked and serve at once.

INDEX

RECIPE CREDITS

Valerie Aikman-Smith
Korean sticky ribs
Salt and pepper squid
Spicy pork satay skewers

Caroline Artiss
Vietnamese chicken and quinoa
    bites

Jordan Bourke
Charred shrimp with nam jim
Courgette/zucchini onion bhajis
Japanese okonomiyaki pancakes
Smoked mackerel sushi rolls
Tempura vegetables and shrimp
Vietnamese shrimp-stuffed

Dunja Gulin
Vegan maki and California rolls
Vegan temaki rolls with seed pâté

Tori Haschka
Sashimi and cucumber bites

Carol Hilker
Asian caramel wings
Chinese egg rolls
Kung pao wings
Sake wings
Sticky teriyaki wings
Thai green curry wings

Thai peanut chicken wings
Thai-style fried chicken wings
Vietnamese summer rolls

Vicky Jones
Indian lentil and rice dosas
Korean moong pancakes

Jackie Kearney
Cauliflower and kale pakoras
Oothapam
Sweet 'n' sour popcorn tofu

Jenny Linford
Crispy chicken wontons
Korean kimchi pancake
Mushroom pakoras
Mushroom-filled lettuce cups
Steamed Asian black garlic scallops
Taiwanese-style garlic pork bao
Yakitori-glazed mushroom and
    chicken skewers

Loretta Liu
Barbecue pork puffs
Beef bulgogi puffs
Chinese turnip cake
Chinese vegetable clamshell buns
Fried shrimp and scallop bao
Golden pumpkin and leek dumplings
Hoisin duck puffs

Lotus leaf rice dumplings
Mushroom puff pastry dumplings
Pork and cabbage shumai
Pork and leek jiaozi
Red Thai curry and lentil bao
Salmon and mushroom dumplings
Scallop and crab dumplings
Shrimp and mango wontons
Spicy chicken and shrimp
    dumplings
Traditional shrimp dumplings

Uyen Luu
BBQ pork-belly skewers
Rice rolls with pork and shrimp
Smoked duck summer rolls
Vietnamese BBQ spareribs
Vietnamese pork-stuffed crêpes

Dan May
Green chilli/chile bhajis

Nitisha Patel
Amritsari fish pakoras
Tandoori-spiced lamb chops

Louise Pickford
Beef bulgogi and rice noodle wraps

Milli Taylor
Chinese duck breast pancakes

PHOTOGRAPHY CREDITS

Ed Anderson 87

Peter Cassidy 13, 51, 70, 82, 83

Helen Cathcart 73

Tara Fisher 1, 53–57, 79, 118

Jonathan Gregson 139

Louise Hagger 2, 6, 10, 16–45, 49,
    58, 59

Erin Kunkel 78, 115

William Reavell 66–69, 98, 107

Toby Scott 92, 119, 120, 123, 127,
    128, 132, 135

Ian Wallace 4, 7, 50, 88, 104, 105,
    110–112

Kate Whitaker 95, 100, 121, 133,
    136, 137

Isobel Wield 96

Clare Winfield 3, 5, 11, 14, 46, 47,
    61–65, 74–77, 80, 81, 84, 85, 91,
    99, 102, 103, 108, 109, 116, 117,
    124, 131, 140, endpapers